QUEEN CITY of the NORTH

Dawson City, Yukon
A Pictorial History

Joseph Ladue, the founder of Dawson City.

SAWMILL OWNED BY JOSEPH LADUE, FOUNDER OF. DAWSON CITY.

QUEEN CITY of the NORTH

Dawson City, Yukon

A Pictorial History

by Stan B. Cohen

Between 1896 and 1899, Dawson had grown from a mud flat to the largest Canadian city north of Vancouver and west of Winnipeg, with a population of more than 30,000. For one year—from June 1898 to July 1899—it was one of the grandest cities in North America, where one could do or buy most anything that one had money for. YA

LIBRARY OF CONGRESS
CATALOG CARD NO. 90-60030

ISBN 0-929521-31-5

First Printing April 1990

PRINTED IN CANADA

Typography: Arrow Graphics & Typography
Cover Design: Kirk Johnson

About the Author

Stan Cohen, a native of West Virginia, is a graduate geologist who spent two summers working in Alaska as a geologist for the U.S. Forest Service. Since 1976 he has spent part of every summer in Alaska and the Yukon researching and writing about the North Country. He established Pictorial Histories Publishing Co., Inc., in 1976 and has since written 38 history books and published over 120. His other North Country titles include: *The Streets Were Paved With Gold; the Forgotten War, Vol. I and II; the Trail of '42; Gold Rush Gateway; Yukon River Steamboats; Rails Across The Tundra; Alaska's Wilderness Rails; Top Cover For America; Journey to the Koyukuk; The Great Alaska Pipeline; The Opening of Alaska; Flying Beats Work* and *The White Pass & Yukon Route*. He lives in Missoula, Montana, with his wife, Anne.

PICTORIAL HISTORIES PUBLISHING CO.
713 South Third West, Missoula, Montana 59801

Introduction

I first visited Dawson City in the fall of 1963. I took a Labor Day weekend trip over the Top of the World Highway from my summer job on the Kenai Peninsula in Alaska examining placer gold deposits for the U.S. Forest Service. I had heard a few stories about the Klondike Gold Rush but really knew very little about it. Little did I know that this one trip would influence my life 13 years later.

Dawson, as I remember it, was then just awakening from a long sleep and emerging as a tourist site. The Federal Department of Northern Affairs and Natural Resources had just moved in a few years before and rebuilt the Palace Grand Theater and a few other buildings were either restored or in the process of restoration. But for the most part the town remained in a time frame of perhaps 30 years before. There were even a few stores that were closed but still stocked with merchandise from many years before.

It was a quaint town in those days, ghostly but yet vibrant. Some gold mining kept the town alive, helped along by a small but steady stream of tourists coming to the far north to soak up some of the past color and lore of the gold rush.

I was not to return to the area until 1976 but that first visit never left my mind. During several career changes from geologist to ski shop owner to book author and publisher, I always wanted to return to the North. I got my chance in the summer of 1976 when my wife and I retraced the steps of the 1897-99 gold prospectors from Seattle, up the Inside Passage to Skagway over both the Chilkoot and White passes and then by car to Dawson. This fantastic trip was done for a book I published in 1977—*The Streets Were Paved With Gold*—which is still in print. Since then I have also written and published books on Skagway, the White Pass and Yukon Route and Yukon River steamboats.

These books, including this, my newest, have allowed me to visit the Yukon every summer since 1976. The Yukon and in particular, Dawson, seem to draw me like a magnet and perhaps this allows me to live out a fantasy, to be one of those prospectors of so long ago.

This is certainly not the definitive history of Dawson, yet I believe it is the most comprehensive book published to date of the visual, historical record. By using a good selection of historic and modern photographs I have tried to give the reader a sense of the magnitude of Dawson and the gold rush days and the many years that followed down to the present.

Parks Canada has done a wonderful job in preserving the atmosphere of old-time Dawson. This has not been an easy task. Not only is adequate funding a constant issue, but the harsh climate, the frozen soil, the ever-present threat of fire and that of occasional floods are major problems to overcome. There have been some notable reconstruction successes, and there are more on the horizon. The Klondike Visitors Association can also take a great amount of credit for upgrading facilities and providing many attractions for the visitor. And we cannot overlook the people of Dawson who, along with the territorial government, have shown immense pride in the "Queen City of the North."

I wish to thank my friends Kathy and Michael Gates of Dawson for their many years of help and for reviewing this manuscript. Thanks also to other staff members of the Canadian Parks Service in Dawson and Winnipeg for their help and guidance. And, as usual, the staff of the Yukon Archives in Whitehorse was very cooperative as was the entire staff of the Dawson City Museum. A special thanks goes to my friend Wayne Towriss of Whitehorse who copied some of the photos used in this book. Other photos were obtained from the University of Washington Library, Special Collections, the Anchorage Museum of History & Art, the University of Alaska Archives, the Alaska State Library, the Vancouver Public Library, the Provincial Archives of British Columbia, the Glenbow Archives in Calgary, other collections acknowledged and my own collection of photos and original written material. I must also give special thanks to Dick North who provided much information on Jack London's story in this book. And my last thanks go to all my bookstore and museum accounts in the Yukon who have stuck with me all these years and through sales of my books have allowed me to follow my own Trail of '98 these many years.

Jacquelyn McGiffert of Missoula edited my manuscript, Arrow Graphics of Missoula typeset the book and Kirk Johnson of Missoula produced the cover graphics.

—Stan Cohen

FIRST DIRECT NEWS OF THE SERIOUS SITUATION IN DAWSON CITY.

SUFFERING IN YUKON COUNTRY.

John D. McGillivray, of the Herald's Expedition to the Klondike, Sends the First Report from Gold Fields.

MINERS ADVISED TO LEAVE DAWSON.

Canadian Officials Post a Warning Notice to All Who Are Not Supplied with Food.

HUNDREDS GO DOWN RIVER.

Men and Women Start in Small Boats for Circle City in Hope of Finding Provisions.

CRIMINALS OUT OF PRISON.

Prospect of Starvation Causes Crimes and Police Cannot Take Care of Men Who Are Arrested.

John D. McGillivray, mining expert, and Max Newberry, special artist, of the HERALD's expedition to the Klondike gold fields, have arrived in Dawson City after a tedious trip up the Yukon.

Mr. McGillivray's letter to the HERALD is the first report sent out of the gold district by a newspaper correspondent. In it he describes the true situation in the gold camps. As he predicted in his former letters from points along the Yukon River, lack of food has caused great distress among the miners.

Many persons have left Dawson for points further down the river where they could get food. The Canadian officials warned all who were without a plentiful supply of provisions against remaining in Dawson.

Lack of provisions soon caused an epidemic of thefts, which resulted in murders. Persons arrested cannot be cared for, as the police have no provisions for them. Murderers and thieves are generally put into boats and started down the river.

HUNDREDS LEAVE DAWSON.

Klondikers Go Down River to Save Themselves from Starvation.

DAWSON CITY, Northwest Territory, Oct. 14, 1897, via SEATTLE, Wash., Sunday.—I arrived here more than a fortnight ago, after having poled and tracked for a distance of 300 miles up the Yukon River.

The situation in Dawson, and, in fact, all along the Yukon, has become distressing. There are about two thousand persons in Dawson for the winter. Two weeks ago Captain Hansen, manager of the Alaska Commercial Company, arrived here, having come with all haste from Fort Yukon to warn the people of their danger, and since then seven or eight hundred men and a few women have been taken down the river in small boats.

The steamer Weare arrived two weeks ago with about two hundred tons of freight. This raised false hopes, and, to make matters worse, the Bella was reported to be on her way up. The Canadian officials decided that some steps must be taken to relieve the situation. Captain Constantine, of the mounted police; H. W. Davis, Collector of Customs, and Thomas Faucett, Gold Commissioner, issued this notice, which was posted up about town:—

"The undersigned officials of the Canadian government, having carefully looked over the present distressing situation in regard to the supply of food for the winter, find that the stock is not sufficient to meet the wants of the people now in the district, and can see only one way out of the difficulty, and that is an immediate movement down the river of all those who are now unsupplied to Fort Yukon, where there is a large stock of provisions.

Frozen River Ends Hopes.

"Within a few days the river will be closed, and the movement must be made at once. It is absolutely hazardous to build hopes upon the arrival of other boats. It is almost beyond a possibility that any more food will come into this district.

"For those who have not laid in a winter's supply to remain here any longer is to court death from starvation, or, at least, a certainty of sickness from scurvy or other troubles. Starvation now stares every man in the face who is hoping and waiting for outside relief. Little effort and trifling cost will place them all in comfort and safety within a few days at Fort Yukon, or at other points below, where there are now lying stocks of food."

The officials considered the advisability of confiscating all of the boats here, to be distributed among those who might desire to leave. In the meantime several hundred persons made rapid preparation for their departure down the river. It is quite probable that nearly one thousand will go, and they go feeling certain that they will find an abundance of food at or below Fort Yukon.

However, at best they will hardly find more than enough to sustain life through the winter. The highest estimates of the amount of freight down the river do not exceed two thousand tons. With the persons who are now preparing to go or considering the advisability of going, there will be in the lower country probably more than three thousand. Much of the freight is not food, and there is probably not enough to fully supply more than two thousand.

Price of Dogs Increases.

Winter is now setting in and every avenue of relief is closed. No more food can come by the river from St. Michael or over the passes, and the people of the Yukon must settle down to a life of privation without hope of relief from any source until the middle of next June.

Were it possible, many would go out. When the ice has formed it is possible for the hardiest to go out over the pass about January 1. If they go they must carry along for themselves and dogs more food than would be necessary to carry them through the winter.

More than this, such a trip is beyond the reach of many, for the price of dogs is beginning to be beyond the reach of most purses. Those who know the overland routes best say that under no circumstances could food be brought in in sufficient quantities to do any good before the river is cleared of ice again, and that will not be early enough for boats to reach Dawson from the upper river before June 15.

Probably the greatest distress will prevail on the road above Dawson among those who are caught by the flowing ice and compelled to camp and who are poorly supplied with provisions. A large number of these persons have but enough to bring them to Dawson. If they fail to get through there is apt to be considerable distress, and how many there are on the road there is no means of knowing here.

Expect Cattle and Sheep.

There are no supplies at Fort Selkirk, which used to be a supply station for those coming in or going out over the passes. If as many go down the river as is expected now the people in the Klondike district will probably be the best supplied of any in the Yukon with food, for the exodus promises to leave only those who are supplied with food for the winter. More than this, a large number of cattle and sheep, alive or killed on the upper river, will be here in a few days.

Miller Brothers, of Juneau, brought in 150 head of sheep, part of which were killed at Lake Bennett. Their barges are expected to arrive in a few days with all of these. Six hundred and fifty head of sheep or carcasses of mutton have already arrived and are all on the market here. Besides this, three herds of cattle, numbering in all 189 head, are now within a short distance of this place.

It is also reported that Thorp Brothers are bringing 250 head of cattle over the Dalton trail, but many do not believe they will get in this season. Some twenty herding horses, brought in with the cattle and sheep, have been killed for dog meat. It is possible, however, that some of them will be sold, as the horses were in better condition than the cattle and sheep.

Epidemic of Crime.

An epidemic of crime is the result of scarcity of food in Dawson. Within the past week thirty robberies of caches have been reported to the mounted police, and two thieves caught in the act of looting caches have been killed by the owners.

The first was a week ago at a lonely cabin on a bluff, a mile back of town. Three miners who were living there were awakened in the early morning by a noise in the cache. They ran out, one of them carrying a Winchester. A robber was found looting the cache. Without any hesitation the rifle was raised and there was one robber less in Dawson.

The body was buried near the cabin in the dark, and the next day the miners told the mounted police. There was no food to keep them as prisoners. They were told to bury the dead and clear out down river. Names were not asked, and the men, after burying the murdered man on the hillside, took their supplies to the river side and were soon floating down stream in a small boat.

Two days later a robber was shot over in Louse Town, a suburb of Dawson, by one of two owners of a cache. He was robbing shortly after midnight. The police were notified, and the man, who was mortally wounded, was taken to the hospital, where he died the next day.

The two men concerned in the murder are out on parole. It is probable they will be sent down the river. The police can do little else.

Police Short of Rations.

They had not enough rations for all the men here last week and two days ago Captain Harper and twenty more men came down the river without rations. Part of them will go to Forty Mile and live on short rations.

A man caught robbing a cache ten days ago was tried by Captain Constantine and given a year at hard labor. The Captain now sees his mistake. The man had no food and it takes the time of a man to guard him while at work.

I laid a complaint before the Captain a few days ago against a thief who had stolen from me and others. The theft had been committed at Fort Yukon, which is in Alaska. He and a confederate had stolen a ton or more of provisions from the river steamers on which they came up, one as a steward and the other as a cook.

This has been confiscated and the two men have been sent down the Yukon on a small boat with food enough to carry them as far as Fort Yukon.

Not a night passes that one or more caches are not robbed. Locks are scarce and the poorest kind of padlocks will sell for an ounce or more of gold. Hundreds of men stand guard over their property every night.

Few cabins along the creeks or in the town are ever left without some one on watch. Most of the miners have expressed determination to shoot any one caught robbing. At present the river is running clear of ice, but within a few days it will be closed again, and then it will be out of the question to send away any of these evildoers.

Miners Robbed Systematically.

The miner is proverbially careless of his gold, but probably he has never allowed himself to be robbed systematically and with his own knowledge and consent more than along the Yukon.

The recognized value of dust all up and down the river, from whatever mine or district it may come, is $17 an ounce in making purchases or in other ordinary transactions. Yet if he pays at a store, barber shop or saloon $2 there will be taken from his sack one-eighth of an ounce, or $2.12½.

There is no check or guard against dishonest weights. Again, reputable traders may use incorrect weights unwittingly. I had $300 in dust weighed out at Circle City on one of the largest scales in town. Upon paying it over it was weighed on another pair and showed $298.50.

In Circle City one of the passengers of the steamer Bella obtained $10 at the Alaska Commercial Company's store, and spent $5 in drinks. Returning to the store he found that he had $4.25 left. Another took $10, paid out $5 in one payment, and the balance weighed $4.75.

Sweepings Pan Out Gold.

Yesterday, to test the matter, I had five dollars weighed on the best scales in Dawson. I made three payments at different places of one dollar each, and two of fifty cents, and then had less than five cents left. I had lost nearly a dollar out of five. Much gold is lost in paying out and handling.

At Circle City I saw boys scrape up and wash the sweepings from the stores and saloons several mornings. In one case $3.50 was obtained from one panning, while they seldom found less than twenty-five cents.

The stores of the trading companies, when business is brisk, make out of overweights on taking gold several hundred dollars daily above their cash balance. This information comes from the companies themselves.

Captain Healey, of the North American Transportation and Trading Company, in pointing out the need for coin here for making change, says that the United States and Canadian governments could send in many millions of silver to advantage.

The Indians are distrustful of gold dust and will not keep it, but immediately on receipt of it pay it out in trade. The value of gold from the different districts varies considerably. Few assays have been made, but they indicate that gold as base as $15.25 and as fine as $19 an ounce is found.

Captain Constantine has recommended to the Canadian government that an assay office be established here and gold be run into bullion and its actual value paid to the miners in Dominion bills. Under existing conditions the gold output of this district goes to the United States.

New Mining Laws to Stand.

Word has been brought to Dawson that the Canadian government, in reconsidering the new mining laws, has decided to let them stand, and has sent on men to enforce them and collect the royalty.

No formal protest was sent by the miners while these laws were under consideration, for they could not believe that laws so manifestly unfair and uncalled for would be passed and put in force. Until a copy was received three weeks ago by the Gold Commissioner, reports as to the terms of the new laws were regarded as canards.

The Gold Commissioner himself, on receiving the law, pigeonholed it to await the arrival of Major Walsh, who, he was informed, was on his way with fuller powers. Now Captain Harper, of the mounted police, has arrived, bringing, besides twenty police, five surveyors. The advance guard of the Canadian government administrative outfit is now on its way to enforce the laws and collect the royalty.

There was no food here for the surveyors, and they have been sent down the river to Forty Mile. The news was first learned by a few mine owners late this afternoon, and to-night the food question is forgotten and dozens of men who have been hastening men and supplies out to their properties to begin the winter's work are recalling orders and preparing to stop as much work as possible.

Taxation May Close Mines.

The secretary of the Mine Owners' Association yesterday estimated that the mines of El Dorado Creek would produce $4,000,000. He says that the proposed royalty will close them all or that the owners will do only enough work to hold their leases from the government. Some of the Canadians who are large owners talk of rebellion, and say that they will not submit to what they call an outrage.

One thing is certain, the Klondike is dead, and there can be no prospecting in the Yukon district. A meeting will be called immediately, and it is proposed to send on over the first ice a representation to Ottawa. When the Gold Commissioner received a copy of the law three weeks ago it was understood that Major Walsh was coming in with power to enforce or modify it, and a meeting was held at which a commission was appointed to draft a memorial to be presented to him to be forwarded.

Now it is understood that the law will be enforced if an appeal to Ottawa direct is not made immediately. The three provisions that are now objectionable are:—

First—A royalty tax of ten per cent on the gross yield of each mine up to $26,000 per year, and twenty per cent of that part in excess of the $26,000.

Second—Creek claims hereafter located shall be but 100 feet in length, instead of 500 feet, as under the old law.

Third—Alternate claims shall be reserved by the government and sold at auction.

As to the first provision—the royalty—it may be said safely, under present conditions not one out of the ten producing mines in the district could be worked at a profit and pay it. Nearly all the mines on Bonanza are to be worked on lays, or will be if this provision does not discourage the lay holder.

Few Can Afford to Pay Royalty.

The owners have given lays rather than pay wages, and the lay holders expect to make only wages or a little more. Many mines or interests in mines have been purchased for sums which the owners can never expect to recover and pay the royalty. With wages at $1 or $1.50 an hour few mines will return ten or twenty per cent profit out of the gross yield.

Outside of the few mines on El Dorado Creek, not exceeding forty, and half a dozen in Bonanza and a few in Hunker, say fifty in all, of the mines can make twenty per cent profit, or even ten per cent at present prices of supplies and rates of wages. Men owning low grade mines will not work them, and an exodus may be expected to the other side of the line.

Hunker, Dominion, Henderson and all other creeks which have been promising will be deserted. The mine owners assert, and with good reason, that the Canadian government is not acting in good faith and is, in fact, violating a contract. These men have been induced to come in here and locate and open up mines upon certain conditions. One of the clauses of the lease under which they hold is this:—

"The said Minister of the Interior hereby grants to the said John Doe, for one year, the exclusive privilege to enter on said claim for mineral working thereof, and the exclusive right to all the proceeds realized therefrom."

The clause of the new law cutting down the size of claims to be located to 100 feet in length will prevent any further prospecting. On opening up a mine the owner is at heavy expense for what may be called permanent improvements.

First Expenses Are Heavy.

If it is a claim that may be sluiced he must build cabins, put up sluices, cut a drain, put in a dam, buy tools, &c. Besides this he will have sunk prospect shafts to locate the pay channel. Then, his time lost in prospecting for a claim should be considered. There are few claims from which enough money has been taken in the first 100 feet to pay for all this—certainly none outside of El Dorado, and one or two on Bonanza.

Alex McDonald and Fred Hutchison, both Canadians and large mine owners, asked to-day why it was that the Canadian government had not taken the trouble to send in here to report upon the conditions agents who might be presumed to know something of mining. It may be said that every one of the government officials now here regard the new regulations as ill advised.

"The least that the Canadian government can do is to suspend these laws until it makes an examination through competent men," said McDonald. "So far no man competent to judge of the conditions has been sent in here for the government."

JOHN D. McGILLIVRAY.

GOLD MINING ALONG THE YUKON.

Mrs. Elizabeth Brough accompanied a party of prospectors over a very rough trail, thirty miles, to Hunter Creek, where she staked claim No. 68. After it was staked an old miner shovelled a panful of gravel from the creek bed and "panned out" several "colors," or particles of gold.

[Drawn by Max Newberry, Special Artist of the HERALD's Expedition to the Klondike Gold Fields.]

MANOOK.

Alaskan Indian Who Discovered Gold on the Creek Which Now Bears His Name.

BROUGHT BACK TREASURE.

Twenty-Five Miners Return from Dawson with Drafts and Dust.

SEATTLE, Wash., Sunday.—The steamer City of Seattle arrived here to-day from Skaguay, Alaska. She had on board twenty-five men, who left Dawson on October 14, coming out over the Dalton trail.

The passengers brought $60,000 in drafts and $200 in dust and nuggets.

HUNGRY MINERS STOP STEAMERS.

The Portus B. Weare and the Bella Compelled to Leave Food in Circle City.

WILLING TO PAY FOR IT.

Miners' Only Demand Is That They Shall Not Be Prevented from Buying Necessities.

FORCE OVERAWES OFFICIAL.

Men Armed with Shotguns and Rifles Appear on a Bluff and Support Committee's Demands.

CIRCLE CITY, Alaska, Sept. 30, via SEATTLE, Wash., Sunday.—Armed with rifles and intrenched behind wood piles and cabins, a large force of miners of the Birch Creek district ten days ago compelled the North American Trading and Transportation Company's steamer, Portus B. Weare, to discharge sufficient of her cargo to meet their pressing wants.

The steamer, in charge of the manager of the company, E. E. Weare, and carrying 200 tons of freight, had passed the Yukon flats, and it was the intention to stop at Circle City only long enough to discharge provisions for the company mess. She had no sooner made fast, however, than she was boarded by a committee of six, chosen at a miners' meeting held the day before, and a demand for provisions was made on Mr. Weare. The chairman of the committee said the miners were prepared to pay any price the company might exact. He said the goods could be placed in the hands of the company's agent and the committee would guarantee payment.

Armed Men Threaten Steamer.

The demand met with a direct refusal from Mr. Weare, who declared that the cargo must go directly to Dawson City, as much of it was in bond. The chairman made a peculiar signal, and immediately fifty men, armed with rifles and shotguns, ranged themselves on a bluff, commanding the boat. Mr. Weare was told that if he attempted to put a man in the pilot house his action would be resented and the man would be compelled to leave the wheel.

Mr. Weare declined further conference, and the miners began unloading and checking out the cargo. This brought Mr. Weare to a realization of the fact that the miners were determined, and after several conferences, during which the men offered advantageous terms for the settlement of the trouble and were rebuffed, the work of unloading proceeded.

There were several clashes in the afternoon between miners and peace officials, but no direct violence was offered. Mr. Weare capitulated at five o'clock, and agreed to treat with the miners in the morning. An armed guard was left aboard the boat, and the residents of the city returned to the beach. Mr. Weare agreed in the morning to allow everything that had been taken ashore to remain and to land enough more to supply the immediate wants of the camp. He also agreed to give a rebate on all provisions it would be necessary to freight from Fort Yukon to complete the winter's supply.

Complaint of Continued Injustice.

"The men were forced to this by the unjust treatment they have been subjected to for the last two or three years," said a leading miner to me. "Even before the Klondike strike we were compelled to freight with dogs from points above or below at an enormous expense. It has been almost impossible since then to get a boat to land anything here. Previous to the Klondike strike this district was the principal producer on the river, and to us the companies looked for their profits. We have been promised time and again fair treatment, and have finally lost patience. Our action is but a natural result of their indifference to our wants.

"I have been living for a week on flour and water, with an occasional salmon or piece of moose meat. We cannot work our claims unless we can get something more substantial than promises."

The Weare was allowed to proceed to Dawson City at eleven A. M., September 21.

Another Steamer Held Up.

The steamer Bella, which came up the river a few days after the Weare, fared no better. It had no orders to leave supplies here, but she was held up by determined miners, and fifty tons of food were brought ashore and placed in the Alaska Commercial Company's store to be sold at the usual prices to those in need of food. Guards were placed on the boat to see that nothing was stolen. Captain Dixon, one of the most popular men on the river, could not stop the miners.

"When I saw they were simply hungry men who insisted on being fed," he said to me, "I could do nothing. They were reasonable and took off only enough to keep them alive. What they took from the Weare and from the Bella will barely feed them for eight months. I suppose, too, they will have to feed the hungry men passing through during the winter."

Army Officer Addresses Miners.

Captain Ray, of the United States Army, who was on board, on his way from Fort Yukon to call on Captain Constantine, of the Canadian mounted police, in Forty Mile, addressed the miners, and asked their authority for taking goods off a common carrier. He was told there were in Circle City nearly two hundred men, all producers, who had not food enough to keep them alive through the year, and that they did not purpose to starve while they had plenty of money to pay any price the company might ask. Captain Ray asked them to take no more than enough to barely carry them through and to remember others were likely to be short of food in Dawson.

JOHN D. McGILLIVRAY.

PATHETIC SCENES IN DAWSON

Two Steamers Bring Little Food and Then Hundreds Leave.

DAWSON CITY, Northwest Territory, Oct. 14, 1897, via SEATTLE, Wash., Sunday.—Some pathetic scenes have been witnessed on the water front of Dawson City during the last two weeks. The people had waited for weeks for the arrival of a steamer with food, and had been told that no relief could be expected when the steamer Weare hove in sight late in the evening of September 28, and the town

FIRST REPORT ON KLONDIKE BY AN IMPARTIAL MINING EXPERT.

ACTUAL SITUATION IN THE KLONDIKE

John D. McGillivray, the Herald's Expert, Tells of Chances Prospectors Have for Success in the Gold Fields as Miners or Laborers.

ONLY ONE RICH DISCOVERY HAS BEEN MADE

Men Who Rush to the New El Dorado Find That There Are No Mines for Them and That Under Present Conditions Not More Than Half of Them Can Obtain Work.

John D. McGillivray, the HERALD'S correspondent in the Klondike gold region, who is an expert in gold mining, sends another letter to the HERALD telling of the conditions which gold seekers are confronted with in the new El Dorado.

Mr. McGillivray had been studying the situation in Dawson city and the mines for two weeks or more when the letter was written. He calls particular attention to the fact that all the claims on the richest of the gold creeks have already been taken up and that new comers must prospect for themselves or work as laborers in the mines already opened.

The situation, as to the number of men the mines will support, the quantity of food and the chances of making living wages by hard work, is also gone into in detail.

MANY REGRET WILD RUSH.

Men in Klondike Realize That They Must Undergo Many Hardships.

DAWSON CITY, Northwest Territory, Oct. 17, 1897.—Nine out of ten of the numbers who have come to the Yukon in the rush now wish they were back home. They have learned that there are no mines for them and that wages at $15 a day is a myth. It should be borne in mind by all who think of coming here that with all the prospecting that has been done by hundreds of experienced men during the past ten years only one discovery has been made of ground that will under present conditions pay large profits, and that is on Bonanza, and its tributary, Eldorado Creek.

None who come here now may hope to obtain mines on these creeks, except at exorbitant prices. There have been many stampedes of late, but there have been stampedes for years along the Yukon upon the reports of rich discoveries, and all who have joined in these rushes have been disappointed with the exception of those who came to the Klondike.

There has been a rush to Munook Creek, and locations are selling there for as much as $5,000 each. This is all based on the fact that one man found a good prospect at the bottom of a shaft last spring, and the further fact that food is more accessible there than elsewhere.

May Be Another Eldorado.

It is possible that Munook will turn out to be another Eldorado, but no more probable than that Coal Creek, Mission Creek, American, Nation, Henderson or a dozen others will turn out rich. The chances of finding another creek as rich as Eldorado are very small.

One may be found—a dozen may. It is possible that another Cripple Creek will be found in Colorado, but that is no reason why all the world should rush to Colorado.

There is nothing left for those who are now coming, or are here and waiting for some one to start a stampede, to do but go out prospecting or work for wages. Wages will probably be $1 an hour. If they shall be $1.50 an hour the mine owners say that they will not employ many men.

In winter men can work but seven or eight hours a day. Fifteen dollars a day has seldom been earned at wages except in a few summer claims.

The only other alternative is to go out prospecting. To simply live here involves hard work. But to prospect means hardship and privation that none but the most hardy can endure.

One must carry his tools, bedding, stove and food on his back over the most wretched roads, or after the winter has set in pay freight at the rate of ten or fifteen cents a pound. In summer freight is from twenty-five cents to $1 a pound from Dawson or Circle City or Forty Mile out to the creeks. To the prospector this is prohibitive, for to move out to one of the creeks with a small outfit takes a long time. One must build a cabin or sleep in a tent with the thermometer registering at times seventy or eighty degrees below zero.

Compared with California.

Prospecting itself when on the ground involves much more labor for the results than in any other mining district in the world. It is seldom that the pay dirt is to be found uncovered, and shafts must be sunk to bedrock by thawing the ground with fires and digging out.

The pay channel, as it is called, is generally from fifteen to fifty or sixty feet wide. In order to locate it prospect shafts must be sunk at short distances across the valley of the creek, which may be from one hundred to a thousand feet wide.

A season may be lost in prospecting in one or two rows of holes. They may be sunk where there is no good pay in the creek, while rich ground may be found later a few hundred yards above or below.

In California in early days prospecting along the creeks was simple and easy. The pay was in or near the creek beds. One could follow up a stream and pan out a little here and there until he came to rich ground. To prospect miles of creeks was the work of a few days.

Here it is all different. In the first place, the gold is not in the beds of the present streams nor in such bars as bordered the California creeks, but in the "till" or ground moraines of ancient glaciers left there ages before the streams began to cut their present channels, and a week's hard work is necessary to reach it through the muck and gravel that covers it.

A man could prospect miles of creeks in California in those days in a week easier and more thoroughly than he could a hundred yards of one of these creeks in a year.

To understand this it must be remembered that the gold of the California streams was probably first crushed and milled from the quartz veins of the Sierras by glaciers; that it was then washed by the ancient rivers with the gravel such as is found and being worked now by drifting at a depth of hundreds of feet in places under lava caps on the divides between the present rivers.

Great Riches on the Creeks.

Those ancient river channels were later cut into and in part washed away by modern rivers and creeks, and along them the gold has been found in their bottoms and in the bars and benches along their sides and formed by them.

From these deposits more than five hundred millions of dollars in gold was taken within ten years after Marshall made his discovery in Sutter's mill race at Coloma.

The quartz was crushed and the gold concentrated by the glaciers, further concentrated by the ancient rivers and still further concentrated by the modern streams.

Here it is different. Nature has had only the first of these forces at work—that of the glacier. Practically all the rich gold bearing deposits of the Klondike district on Eldorado and Bonanza creeks are but the ground moraine of great glaciers of the ice age.

In all parts of the Yukon country are to be found alluvial deposits in the shape of bars and benches, which contain gold, it is true, but so far none has been found to compare in richness with the gold bearing deposits of Eldorado and Bonanza creeks, which have been the cause of this useless influx of thousands from the outside world.

The best proof of the fact that there are already here many more persons than can hope ever to obtain claims without going far away is in the figures of the Gold Commissioner as to the number of locations that have been made. The whole length, practically, of every creek within a distance of forty miles, and in some directions more, has been located.

Where the Gold Comes From.

These creeks include Eldorado, Bonanza, Hunker and other tributaries of the Klondike River, as far up as All Gold, fifty miles away; Sulphur, Dominion and Quartz, branches of Indian; Henderson, a branch of Stewart, and Bryant, Montana, Deadwood and Adams, branches of the Yukon.

Yet all these locations, together with a few in the Forty Mile district, do not exceed in number 1,800. But under the mining laws a man may locate one claim in each division of the Yukon district. There are eight divisions, and many men have claims in several of these. So it is safe to say that about one thousand men own all these claims.

There are in Dawson and in the mines of these districts at the present time certainly over four thousand five hundred persons, and probably five thousand. Besides this there are, of those who came in late by St. Michael and those who went down to Fort Yukon in order to obtain food, certainly not less than one thousand, who intend to come here as soon as navigation opens in the spring.

Hundreds Coming Over the Trail.

There are coming into Dawson from up the river daily from twenty to forty men in small boats. It is said by those who have come in last that there are at least one thousand men on the road who have crossed the passes and will winter on the trails and come in early in the spring.

From all indications this is a low estimate. In other words, there are here, or near here and to come as soon as roads open, seven thousand men, and there are mines in the district for one thousand. The other six thousand can only hope to work for wages or go long distances from here to prospect.

Of all the mines located not more than two hundred and fifty have been proved to be of value under present conditions, and of these many will not be worked full handed until wages are still further reduced. So far as can be learned from the mine owners themselves, about one thousand men will be employed in the mines if wages are $1 an hour. Then as many more will work on lays.

In addition to these not more than one thousand will work on their own claims prospecting, developing or mining them, making in all about three thousand men employed in the mines.

Many May Not Have Supplies.

Yet it is probable that not so many will have supplies of provisions to last them until spring. Of the rest of the population of the district 1,500 or more will be idle, unless they move out and prospect. When the winter work is over there will be employment for far less men in summer or sluice mining, and with those coming there will be but a small proportion of the men here employed unless new mines are discovered.

There have been during the last decade many thousand men in the Yukon country prospecting and mining all the way from the Hootalingna River to the Koyu-Kuk, a distance of eight hundred miles in a straight line. Hundreds have gone away poor in pocket and broken in health by the rigors of the climate, hardships and privations.

Up to two years ago but one of all these men had made a respectable amount at mining, and that was only $50,000, made by John Miller, who in three years took that out of his mine on Miller Creek in Forty-Mile district.

Since then probably half a dozen men have made that much in the Birch Creek district. There are in the Klondike district but few mines that will do better, as far as is known now. There are not more than 250 mines in the district that have been proven to be of sufficient value to work at a profit under present conditions.

All this does not offer much encouragement to those coming here. Yet the Yukon country has been heralded to the world as one of the greatest of mining districts. It certainly is, but the bulk of its yield of bullion will come from mines that to-day and under present conditions cannot be worked at a profit.

Combine to Reduce Wages.

The high prices, the scarcity of the necessaries of life and the difficulties of travel and transportation make it impossible for poor men or men of small means to work any but exceedingly rich claims.

The cost of working is from $5 to $20 per cubic yard. Similar deposits are worked under similar conditions and by almost the same methods in Siberia for fifty cents per cubic yard. Ground worth there $5 per cubic yard pays a high profit. Here it cannot be touched.

The mine owners held a meeting two weeks ago at which it was decided to pay only a dollar an hour wages from October 1 to June 1, 1898. Wage earners have held several meetings, at which they have agreed to stand out for $1.50 an hour, and in two cases have compelled men who were working for $1 an hour to quit.

A meeting was held by them yesterday, and it was determined to stand out. Neither side up to the present time could tell its strength. The mine owners are better organized, and many of them are in a position to let their mines lie idle rather than pay the higher rates.

At Circle City last winter the claim owners were trying to reduce wages to eighty cents an hour, when the Klondike miners offered $1.50. After the dumps had been made ready for sluicing and stripping was begun for summer work a number of claim owners on Eldorado attempted to reduce the rate to $1. An informal combine was formed for the purpose, but it happened that many of these men had purchased their claims, paying down a little cash and agreeing to pay the balance by July 1 out of the ground.

Much Less Gold Than Reported.

The days went by and the wage earners refused to work. Soon the lockout was broken and the men went to work at $1.50 an hour. A very few of the mines, and those are nearly all on Eldorado, can pay $1.50 an hour and leave themselves any profit.

While the amount of gold that has been produced by the Klondike mines is very large for the number of cubic yards of ground drifted and sluiced, it is much less than has been generally reported. It is safe to say that the total yield so far has been less than $3,000,000 from Bonanza and Eldorado creeks. Correct figures might show less than $2,500,000.

In making up estimates that have been published it is often that the sums taken down to San Francisco and Seattle by men who have sold their claims have been counted twice, once as part of the amount mined from the claim it came from, and again as mined by the man who received it as pay for his claim.

Again, one hears here of cases where men went away with small sums and have been reported on the outside as having large fortunes. One government official left here in the summer with $1,300. He was reported as having made all the way from $90,000 to $163,000, and he writes back that his poor relations are making life a burden.

Estimated Product of Mines.

Captain Healy, manager of the North American Transportation and Mining Company, estimates that the output of gold from winter drift mining was about $2,000,000, and that from summer sluicing between $500,000 and $700,000.

As to the probable yield for the coming winter and summer, the estimates depend upon the number of men that will be employed. If wages shall not exceed $1 an hour and no rich discoveries draw many men away, Edgar Mizner, the secretary of the Mine Owners' Association, says the yield should reach $10,000,000 from these sources:—

Eldorado, $4,000,000; Bonanza, $4,000,000; Hunker, $1,500,000; small creeks and branches of these and side hill claims, $500,000, and from other creeks in the district, $1,000,000.

Captain Healy says that with wages at $15 a day the yield may not exceed $5,000,000, for in that case the richest mines would make small outputs, while the poorer mines, being worked on lays, would not be affected.

JOHN D. McGILLIVRAY.

KLONDIKERS ARRIVING AT FORT YUKON.

The dogs are preceded by a man on snowshoes, who makes a trail in which the animals walk. Dogs will not pull a sled unless they have a trail. They are kept in line by another man in front of the sled, who steers by means of a "ge stick." This man also does a good part of the pulling.

[Drawn by Max Newberry, Special Artist of the HERALD'S Expedition to the Klondike. Mr. Newberry's pictures are the first sent direct from the gold fields.]

MINERS ON THEIR WAY DOWN THE YUKON RIVER.

After packing their outfits over the passes from Dyea or Skaguay, the miners make their way on foot and by boats on the chain of lakes to the Hootalingua River, a tributary of the Yukon. There they build or buy boats, in which they store their outfits and start on the four hundred mile journey down stream for Dawson City.

[Drawn by Max Newberry, Special Artist of the HERALD'S Expedition to the Klondike.]

STARVING IN DAWSON CITY.

Letter to James R. Keene Points Out the Miseries of the Gold Hunters.

Mr. James R. Keene received the following letter at his office, No. 30 Broad street, yesterday from an expert mining engineer who, with an assistant, was sent to the Klondike region last fall by himself and other capitalists to investigate and report on the situation there. It came late in the afternoon, by way of San Francisco, and Mr. Keene kindly turned it over to the HERALD. It gives the latest detailed description of the conditions prevailing in Dawson City. Mr. Keene asked that the name of the writer, a well known mining expert, be withheld, as it might defeat the object for which he was sent if it were made known. The letter, which follows, is written on rough brown paper, for, as the writer explains, no stationery is obtainable in Dawson:—

The Raid on the Bella.

"DAWSON CITY, N. W. Territory, Oct. 3, 1897.
"JAMES R. KEENE, No. 30 Broad street, New York:—

"DEAR SIR—My last letter, written to you from on board the steamer Bella, after leaving Fort Yukon, under date of September 25, was mailed in Circle City Sunday, September 26, 1897. We reached Circle City Saturday, September 25, at seven P. M. The steamer had barely tied up to her landing, the passengers going on shore in a snow storm, when she was boarded and taken possession of by fifty armed men, who demanded all her stores and supplies for the starving people living in the vicinity of Circle City, some 188 miners. The list they presented called for all the delicacies of the season, but all case goods having been left at Fort Yukon, likewise wines, liquors and cigars, they only found staple articles, namely, flour, bacon, butter, ham and lard.

"The proceedings were very summary. There were about thirty passengers on the boat. The crew, composed of Siwash Indians, left the steamer on her arrival at Circle City. Captain Ray, U. S. A., addressed the mob, but they disposed of him by not paying the slightest attention to his remarks, intimating that 'This was the United States, and to h—ll with the fellows in Canada; that the English government looked out for them, and that they didn't propose to allow food to leave the United States for a foreign country and they starve!'

Seized All the Provisions.

"Accordingly they took about thirty tons of ham, bacon, butter, beans, potatoes—practically all that there was of these articles—and about two hundred sacks of flour. Private property was respected, otherwise we would have had a shooting match on the boat. After cleaning up the vessel armed guards were put on board by the miners, as well as on shore, to prevent any further robbery, though there was really nothing else to take, unless it was private property.

"Sunday morning, about seven o'clock, the Bella left for Forty Mile. From Circle City on the passengers became the crew of the steamer, and at short intervals they were compelled to tie up the boat, go ashore, cut wood and pack it aboard to run the engines. The weather for the remainder of the trip was exceedingly disagreeable, being intensely cold, and snowing the better part of the time. Wednesday night (September 29) Forty Mile, the first port in British territory, was reached. As soon as the steamer was at her moorings she was boarded by a detachmen of the mounted police and the mail sent ashore. There being no cargo to discharge she was ordered up to Fort Cudahy, across the creek from Forty Mile, where she remained that night.

"The Alaska Commercial Company has a trading post at Forty Mile, and the North American Transportation and Trading Company has one at Fort Cudahy. Rumors came thick and fast about starvation in Dawson City and the terrible condition of affairs in general throughout the country. Wednesday night the ice was forming rapidly in the Yukon River, and it looked very much as if the steamer would be unable to face the floating masses as they came down the stream. Thursday morning, although partially frozen in, the steamer started for Dawson City, fifty-three miles away, where she arrived at about half-past five o'clock that evening.

God Forsaken Dawson City.

"A more God forsaken place you never saw. The town lies on a flat on the east side of the river, immediately back of which are hills about five hundred feet high. The river is about three-eighths of a mile wide, and is, I should judge, quite deep. The elevation above sea level is approximately one thousand feet. Where the town is located must have been an old moose swamp. During the summer time it is undoubtedly a regular quagmire.

"Dawson City is very irregularly laid out, the main business portion fronting upon the river about fifteen feet above low water mark. I should judge it would be a hotbed of typhoid fever and every other malarial disease in the summer time, as the thermometer reaches over one hundred degrees Fahrenheit in the shade. At present the ground is covered with bunches of moss, clots of 'nigger heads' and frozen pools of stagnant water, with cabins and tents scattered in every direction. The principal buildings are owned by the Alaska Commercial Company and the North American Transportation and Trading Company. The ground is covered with snow, but I would not be surprised to see a thaw any day, and then everything will be mud up to your knees. At present the river is practically closed—frozen over.

"The population is variously estimated at from three to five thousand. I don't believe there are more than fifteen hundred in town, but a mile above this place there is an encampment, with the classic name of Lousetown, where there are twelve hundred souls. God knows how many more there are up the creeks. All told, the gulches and places dependent upon Dawson may aggregate five thousand persons.

No Food—Whiskey and Death.

"There is no place to eat, no place to sleep, no wood except what is floated down from above the Klondike, and every stick of timber and of wood cut and here in town is already contracted for a dozen times over. There is no glass to make into windows, no sawed lumber on hand except what is owned and contracted for for sluices, and I have not been able to find anything here but capitalists.

"There are fully five hundred loafers in town, who won't work and expect to be fed, and there is no food to feed them with. The police won't arrest them, because they haven't any food with which to feed them. Everything is frozen except the whiskey, and there seems to be an unlimited supply of that article at fifty cents a drink, or $10 per bottle. Champagne is $36 per bottle, and I suppose other beverages are at corresponding figures.

"Pneumonia is getting in its deadly work on the camps, undoubtedly assisted by whiskey, evidently fortified for Russian palates. It is expensive to die here, but dead men come in every day. Frozen potatoes are $1 a pound. Frozen meat (when you get it it has a particular flavor) is $1.50 a pound, wholesale rates, one-half or one-quarter of beef, moose meat the same price; hauling, $5 per hour.

Fabulous Prices for Provisions.

"Five cent cigars cost fifty cents each, and flour, outside of the company's contracts, $125 for a fifty pound sack; candles, $1 apiece. Seventy-five dollars is paid for a five gallon can of coal oil. In fact, none is for sale. Sugar is thirty cents and tea $1 a pound. Coffee, $1 a pound, and not fit for dogs. Ordinary dog meat, which means dried fish, $1 a pound. No man works for less than $15 for nine hours, and confers a very great favor upon you even at that rate. Cordwood, sawed and split, is $50 a cord in the yard. Can't say what it will be before this winter is over.

"Cooking stoves are not to be had for love or money. Some sheet iron ones can be obtained at a cost ranging from $75 to $100. There is one tinner in town working five men, and his orders are thirty days ahead. Sawed lumber, the poorest quality, sells, when you can get it, for $100 for a thousand feet, and flooring is twenty cents a foot. The restaurants are all closed because they cannot buy supplies. Bakeries closed because there is no flour to be obtained. There is no hotel and there are no lodging houses.

"What in the world these people are going to do before the season is over I cannot say. Every building on the main street is either a saloon with a gambling outfit or a dance house. There are only two stores, which belong to the companies, respectively, the Alaska Commercial Company and the North American Transportation and Trading Company. They close at five o'clock, because they have no candles or oil to burn. There is absolutely no place to go. There will be no more steamers here until next July.

Moths to the Gold Candle.

"The people are still coming in over the trail without provisions. The police here are driving every one down the river as he arrives, and the companies will assist in pushing out of town all persons who are not supplied with food. Fortunately I provided myself with the essentials of life before leaving Fort Yukon to the extent of $2,000. At the current rates there is a very small amount for so large a sum of money; $350 would buy it in San Francisco. If to this you add additional freights it will aggregate $2,500.

"I don't know what we will do for light, as we have only one can of oil and one small box of candles, so that when it gets dark all one can do is to retire. The first night after my arrival I chased all over this God-forsaken spot to find a place to sleep in, as I wanted some rest after having enjoyed the oiler's berth on board the Bella—she being a freight boat and not for passengers, and such a hog pen you never saw. Fortunately, with the robes I had and one I bought at Fort Yukon I made up a bed on some slats, and hoped when I reached here to find some place to rest, but there was no such luck in store. I hunted high and low, but found nothing.

"Some cabins on the 'flat,' not fit for pigs, were offered at $100 a month rent. I went back on board the ship thoroughly disgusted as I had no tent and none was to be obtained.

"The next morning, Friday, October 1, we started out and hunted the place from one end to the other. By the merest accident I met a fellow who had just built two cabins. He wouldn't rent under any condition, but would sell for cash. I made a trade with him and bought one of his two cabins, 16 by 20 feet and a lot 25 by 100 feet. There was one window and one door in the cabin, but it looked like a palace alongside of the other places. The location is excellent, away from the rabble, overlooking the river, and above the deadly 'flat.'

Death to Food Thieves.

"The condition of affairs is very precarious here. There is a possibility of there being bloodshed on account of the starving population. The stores sell nothing, and are only partially filling orders in rotation to the best of their ability. I do not dare to move until I am first settled. Caches, where individual supplies are kept, are being nightly robbed, and people are on the qui vive. In several instances thieves have been detected and shot, and I do not dare to leave this place without some one in it, for to lose our supplies at this stage of affairs in Dawson would simply mean—Death. Money can't buy food, and the actual staple of life, flour, is unobtainable.

"The mines are right at hand. One mile above this place the Klondike River enters the Yukon. All travelling must be done on foot or on sleighs drawn by dogs when the river is solidly frozen. It is expected that it will be necessary to freight from Yukon here, 350 miles. Freight cost last year $1.50 per pound; this year the price is $2 a pound.

INDIAN PILOT OF THE P. B. WEARE.

His Name Is Albert Pilot, and He Steered the First Steamboat Up the Yukon River to Dawson City.

[Drawn by Max Newberry, special artist of the HERALD'S Expedition to the Klondike.

TO FRAME ALASKA LAWS.

WASHINGTON, D. C., Tuesday.—Senator Perkins, of California, introduced in the Senate to-day a joint resolution authorizing the President to appoint a commission to draft a code of laws for the Territory of Alaska.

The resolution provides that the commission shall consist of three persons, two of whom shall be residents of Alaska. They are to be paid at the rate of $10 each per day.

Senator McBride, of Oregon, introduced a bill authorizing the Dyea-Klondike Transportation Company to locate and construct a line of transportation from Dyea to Lake Bennett, the line to consist of railways, aerial tramways or wagon roads, as the company may deem proper.

The bill grants 100 feet on each side of the proposed road as right of way. He also introduced a bill granting a similar right of way to the Skaguay and Lake Bennett Tramway Company, from Skaguay over the White Pass to the boundary line of the Northwest Territory.

The Rev. Dr. Hepworth contributes a masterful description of the childhood of Jesus to the CHRISTMAS HERALD, which will be issued next Sunday. It will afford rare pleasure for everybody.

Table of Contents

▼

Photo Acknowledgements

▼

The Klondike Gold Rush was one of the most extensively photographed events of the closing days of the 19th century. This is truly amazing considering how cumbersome the equipment was, how far photographers were from available supplies, and the incredible winter weather and terrain over which they had to travel to get to the gold fields. There are literally thousands of photographs available, mostly made from glass negatives, stored in various archives in both the United States and Canada. Some of the stories of the saving of these collections would make a book in itself.

The source of each photo in this book is acknowledged according to the chart below, and the photographer's name or collection is noted whenever available. There are many photo and historical books published on Dawson City and the entire gold rush spectacle, and some of these are listed in the bibliography.

UW—University of Washington Library, Special Collections, Seattle.
YA—Yukon Archives, Whitehorse.
UAA—University of Alaska Archives, Fairbanks.
ASL—Alaska State Library, Juneau.
AMHA—Anchorage Museum of History & Art, Anchorage.
GA—Glenbow Archives, Calgary, Alberta.
PAC—Public Archives of Canada, Ottawa.
DM—Dawson City Museum and Historical Society, Dawson City.
VPL—Vancouver Public Library, Vancouver.
PABC—Provincial Archives of British Columbia, Victoria.

CHAPTER ONE
EARLY VIEWS

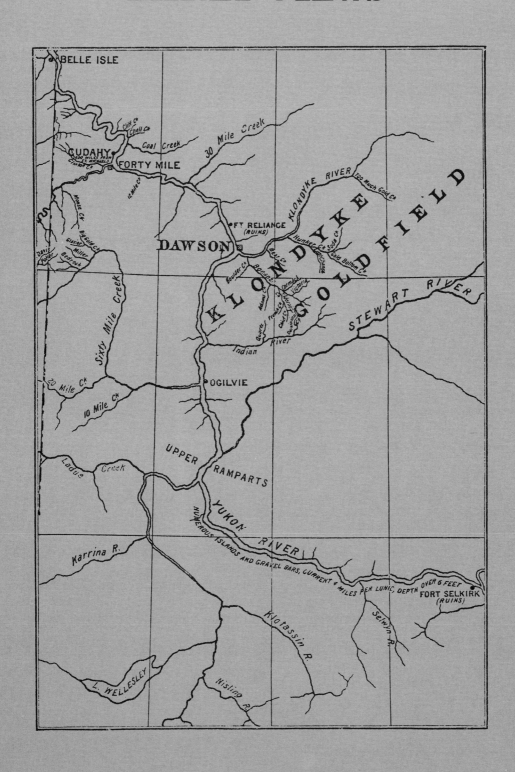

Ladue mill at Dawson about 1898. Ladue in center of picture the other men are his Employes.

#2

DM

Dawson City History

On August 17, 1896 George Carmack discovered gold in a creek he named Bonanza and "The Klondike" became the goal of adventurers and fortune seekers the world over.

Some who came had no intention of "Moiling for Gold" but saw an opportunity to get rich providing services for those who did.

Shortly after Carmack's strike, Joseph Ladue laid claim to a large portion of the flat land at the confluence of the Yukon and Klondike rivers and established a townsite. Born in New York State in 1855, Ladue had been in the Yukon since 1882 as a trader and prospector around the Fort Selkirk and Ogilvie areas.

The town was named for Dr. George M. Dawson, a geologist and first government surveyor to explore the Yukon.

In the winter of 1897, Ladue built a sawmill and a saloon in readiness for the stampede he knew would follow.

By the winter of 1896 the population of Dawson was less than 500, by the summer of 1897, 5,000, and by July 1898 it had swollen to an incredible 30,000.

In one year the small trading post on a mud flat had grown to a bustling mining town of log and tent structures. By late 1898, it had become a modern city of frame buildings, plate glass windows, hotels, theatres, dance halls and even electric light. Dawson became known as the San Francisco of the North and was the largest Canadian city west of Winnipeg.

When word reached Dawson in 1899 of a rich strike in Nome, Alaska, the exodus of the gold hungry miners began.

Consolidation of individual mining claims under corporate bodies and the introduction of gold extraction by dredges after 1900, made for a more stabilized mining industry but a much reduced population. Dawson had become the seat of Territorial Government in 1899 when the Yukon District of the North West Territories became the Yukon Territory. This ensured the continuance of Dawson as a supply and administration centre for the next half century.

With the transfer of the Territorial capital to Whitehorse in 1953, Dawson became a quiet sleepy village. Today, Dawson bustles with tourists and is once again an important supply centre for the placer mining industry.

— Courtesy Klondike Crafts Limited, Whitehorse

Dawson, August 1897, at the height of the first year of the gold rush.
AUTHOR'S COLLECTION

An early view of Dawson.
AMHA

Panorama of the cheechako tent city and a few log cabins in Dawson, 1898. DM

L.A. Nurnberg and friends arriving in Dawson via the "Yukon Flyer," a homemade dory. UW, GOETZMAN

Miners waiting in line to file their claims. Some had to wait for three days. AMHA

Indians selling moose meat, a welcome relief in the fall/winter of 1897 when food was in very short supply. AMHA

Street scene, October 1897. AMHA

Waiting for the first mail of the season, March 3, 1898. The mail left the United States on Nov. 2, 1897. AMHA

Early buildings in Dawson were built of logs, more modern techniques were soon to follow. AMHA

Dawson was still a tent city in early 1898. Tents were set up for every conceivable business, from saloons to dentists' offices. The floors were made out of the boards from the stampeders' boats, and some of the tents were made of the sails. Everyone was on the move, looking for the gold at the end of the rainbow. YA

Stampeders selling their supplies on the waterfront of Dawson. Perhaps they needed money to survive in Dawson or perhaps they were selling out to return south. Either way they were unlikely to strike it rich. Only about 4,000 prospectors who made it to Dawson grew wealthy, and no more than hundred held onto their money in the years after the rush. UW, CURTIS

Looking west in 1897 when Dawson was still mainly a tent town. AMHA

The first mail of 1898 left Dawson on March 5. Six sleds, using a total of 24 dogs, carried 6,000 pounds of letters. AMHA

CHAPTER TWO

FIRE, FLOOD
AND SNOW

Sixty degrees below on Jan. 26, 1905.
UAA, TONI TROSETH COLLECTION

Fire, Flood and Snow

▼

Dawson was a victim of its geographical location and its rapid rise from a moose pasture to a large city. Construction was haphazard, with buildings very close together and prone to rapid spread of fire. The Yukon River posed a constant springtime threat with floods and huge ice jams. Being so far north, Dawson experienced many months of snow cover and extremely cold temperatures. It was a hostile environment that greeted the hundreds of men and women who descended upon the site in 1896 to establish the "Queen City of the North."

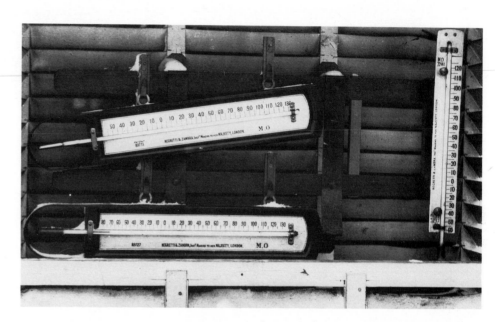

Is it cold in Dawson? This thermometer reads 72° below zero on January 15, 1901. PAC

It is not unusual for temperatures to reach 60 degrees below zero or lower. DM, UW

-8-

A snowstorm on June 16, 1904. Summer seasons are short in this part of North America. The old post office is on the left, the Palace Grand Theater on the right. AUTHOR'S COLLECTION

LAPLANDERS ARRIVING IN DAWSON Y.T. JAN 6th '97

Middle left: In this 1902 photo a group of men with a horse-drawn sleigh are cutting blocks of ice on the Klondike River to transport to Dawson for use in homes and businesses. The Ogilvie Bridge is in the background. DM, LARSS & DUCLOS

Above: During the winter sternwheelers were stored on the Yukon River at Steamboat Slough upriver from Dawson. DM, VOGEE

In January 1897 a group of Laplanders arrived in Dawson with a herd of reindeer to supply fresh meat to the town which was experiencing a lack of food for its burgeoning population. DM, LARSS & DUCLOS

Queen Street during extremely cold temperatures on Jan. 25, 1911.
UAA, LULU FAIRBANKS COLLECTION

This 1898 spring flood inundated the N.W.M.P. stockade.
VPL

Spring break-up would periodically send flood waters into Dawson's streets. The large building is the Bank of British North America, 1989. UW

Spring break-up was always a traumatic time for Dawson's residents. Sometimes the ice would crash into the waterfront buildings causing extensive damage. DM, GOETZMAN

Looking north along Front Street from Queen Street after a flood in 1920. Water and ice residue is still evident in front of the Canadian Imperial Bank of Commerce. The fire department's steam pumper in the background was used to pump water out of the street. YA

Partial panorama of Dawson looking northeast near the waterfront during the spring flood of May 1925.
DM, C. TIDD

Looking north in 1926 along 5th Avenue which has become a shallow river. The men in the canoe are in front of the Administration Building. YA

Flood waters cover the base of the ferry tower in May 1944.
DM, C. HAINES

Flood waters from the Yukon and Klondike rivers were a constant menace to Dawson. This is a 1925 view of the junction of the Yukon and Klondike rivers. YA

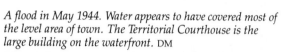

Spring break-up in May 1944 along the Yukon River. YA

A flood in May 1944. Water appears to have covered most of the level area of town. The Territorial Courthouse is the large building on the waterfront. DM

A crowd gathers around the burned-out shell of the Opera House on Front Street. Also visible are the Monte Carlo and the Bank Saloon, April 26, 1899. DM, HEGG

Fire on the hill above Dawson in 1899. PAC

Men dig through the still smoldering debris of the Bank of British North America site. The twisted remains of the bank's vault are at the right, April 26, 1899. VPL, KEIR

•Another view of the bank fire. VPL, KEIR

On Nov. 1, 1901, the Monte Carlo burned along with several other buildings on Front Street. Notice the number of telephone lines coated with ice from the spray of firefighters. PAC

Alaska Commercial Company's buildings and stores are protected from fire by wet blankets on Jan. 10, 1900. Notice the sentry with fixed bayonet on guard in front. GA, LARSS & DUCLOS

Every time a fire burned a gambling hall, enterprising miners would run the remains through a rocker to pick up gold dust inadvertently dropped by the excited miners playing at the gaming tables. UW, GOETZMAN

Cold weather, hot stoves and wooden buildings invited fires. This one started when a dance hall girl threw a lamp at a rival. Since the buildings abutted one another, there was little that could be done to stop the fire, short of blowing up buildings ahead of it to keep fuel away from it. UW, CURTIS

-14-

Ruins of the Yukonia Hotel after the fire on Feb. 22, 1917. Fighting fires at any time of the year was difficult in the early days with limited firefighting equipment and the high risk of wooden buildings built adjacent to each other. In winter the difficulties were compounded by snow and cold temperatures.
AUTHOR'S COLLECTION

A fire on Sept. 23, 1904, burned buildings on Second Avenue. The X indicates the Carnegie Library. VPL

Dawson's earliest horse-drawn fire engine used from 1899 to 1905. PAC

DAWSON FIRE DEPT HOSE WAGGON

A hose wagon and two volunteer firemen on Second Avenue. UAA, BASSOC COLLECTION

Dawson Fire Department, Station No. 1, December 1902. UAA, RALPH MCKAY COLLECTION

CHAPTER THREE
ROBERT SERVICE

Service's cabin as it appeared in the 1940s.
YA, FINNIE COLLECTION

Robert W. Service In Dawson

One of Dawson's well-known personalities and the most noted poet of the North Country, Robert Service, lived in the city from 1908 to 1912. He had migrated to Canada from his native Scotland and finally settled in as a bank clerk in British Columbia after drifting up and down Canada's West Coast. Hearing of the stories of the fabulous 1897-99 Klondike Gold Rush days, Service decided to experience life in the area himself and transferred to the Canadian Bank of Commerce branch in Whitehorse in 1906 and to its Dawson branch in 1908. While in Whitehorse, Service wrote his best-known verse of the Klondike, "The Shooting of Dan McGrew," and his book of verse, *Songs of a Sourdough*. After quitting the bank in 1909 he moved into a two-room log cabin on 8th Avenue.

He lived a spartan life in his little cabin, absorbing in his own words "Yukon lore by every pore." He wrote in this cabin his melodramatic novel, *The Trail of Ninety-Eight*, and his final volume of Yukon verse, *Songs of a Rolling Stone*. Service, known throughout the world as the "bard of the Klondike" set to verse many stories of one of the greatest gold rushes in world history.

The cabin, which may have been constructed as early as the gold rush itself, is typical of the time—logs well chinked with moss to keep out the cold, a double floor with a front porch. It was heated by a wood stove and probably illuminated by coal-oil lamps. The original title was held by Mrs. Matilda Day but it was later acquired by Mrs. Edna Clarke who rented it to Service.

After the poet left Dawson on June 29, 1912, the cabin was never lived in again. In 1917, with Mrs. Clarke reluctantly acquiescing, the Imperial Order of the Daughters of the Empire promoted the cabin as a tourist attraction to raise money for soldiers' relief. After the war the I.O.D.E. continued to promote the cabin, furnishing it in typical miner's style of the gold rush period.

The city of Dawson eventually took over the property and donated it to Parks Canada. It has been restored to the 1909-12 period when Service lived in it, and during the summer months daily readings of Service's poems of the Yukon are held on the lawn.

Service left Dawson in 1912 and became a war correspondent in Europe during World War I. After the war he married a French woman and remained in France. He was forced to flee in 1940 when Germany invaded France and settled in Hollywood, Calif. with his wife and daughter. After the war he returned to France, where he died in 1958. He produced many poems and novels throughout his working life, but never returned to his beloved Yukon.

These three photos of a series of five taken during Service's stay in his cabin show both interior and exterior views. The photographer was A.J. Gillis. DM

Modern-day views of the restored Robert Service cabin on 8th Avenue as it appeared in the 1909-12 era when the poet lived here.

Each summer readings of Service's poems are given on the lawn adjacent to the cabin. Here Tom Bryne entertains a crowd in the summer of 1987.

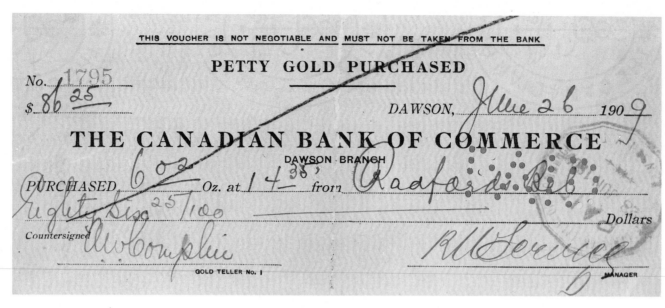

PETTY GOLD PURCHASED

No. 1795

$ 86 25

DAWSON, June 26 1909

THE CANADIAN BANK OF COMMERCE

DAWSON BRANCH

PURCHASED 6 02 Oz. at 14 35 from Radfords Bros

Eighty Six 25/100 ————————————— Dollars

Countersigned A.W.Complin

R.W.Service

GOLD TELLER No. 1

MANAGER

Voucher signed by Service while working for the Canadian Bank of Commerce. GA

The Law of the Yukon

▼

by Robert Service

This is the law of the Yukon, and ever she makes it plain:
"Send not your foolish and feeble; send me your strong and your sane—
Strong for the red rage of battle; sane, for I harry them sore;
Send me men girt for the combat, men who are grit to the core;
Swift as the panther in triumph, fierce as the bear in defeat,
Sired of a bulldog parent, steeled in the furnace of heat.
Send me the best of your breeding, lend me you chosen ones;
Them will I take to my bosom, them will I call my sons;
Them will I gild with my treasure, them will I glut with my meat.
But the others—the misfits, the failures—I trample under my feet.
Dissolute, damned and despairful, crippled and palsied and slain,
Ye would send me the spawn of your gutters—
Go! take back your spawn again.

"Wild and wide are my borders, stern as death is my sway;
From my ruthless throne I have ruled along for a million years and a day;
Hugging my mighty treasure, waiting for man to come,
Till he swept like a turbid torrent, and after him swept—the scum.
The pallid pimp of the dead-line, the enervate of the pen,
One by one I weeded them out, for all that I sought was—Men.
One by one I dismayed them, frighting them sore with my glooms;
One by one I betrayed them unto my manifold dooms.
Drowned them like rats in my rivers, starved them like curs on my plains,
Rotted the flesh that was left them, poisoned the blood in their veins;
Burst with my winter upon them, searing forever their sight, Lashed them with fungus-white faces, whimpering wild in the night;

Staggering blind through the storm-whirl, stumbling mad through the snow,
Frozen stiff in the ice-pack, brittle and bent like a bow;
Featureless, formless, forsaken, scented by wolved in their flight,
Left for the wind to make music through ribs that are glittering white;
Gnawing the black crust of failure, searching the pit of despair,
Crooking the toe in the trigger, trying to patter a prayer;
Going outside with an escort, raving with lips all afoam,
Writing a cheque for a million, driveling feebly of home;
Lost like a louse in the burning...or else in the tented town
Seeking a drunkard's solace, sinking and sinking down;
Steeped in the slime at the bottom, dead to a decent world,
Lost 'mid the human flotsam, far on the frontier hurled;
In the camp at the bend of the river, with its dozen saloons aglare,
Its gambling dens ariot, its gramophones all ablare;
Crimped with the crimes of a city, sin-ridden and bridled with lies,
In the hush of my mountained vastness, in the flush of my midnight skies.
Plague-spots, yet tools of my purpose, so natheless I suffer them thrive,
Crushing my Weak in their clutches, that only my Strong may survive.

"But the others, the men of my mettle, the men who would 'stablish my fame
Unto its ultimate issue, winning me honor, not shame;
Searching my uttermost valleys, fighting each step as they go,
Shooting the wrath of my rapids, scaling my ramparts of snow;
Ripping the guts of my mountains, looting the beds of my creeks,
Them will I take to my bosom, and speak as a mother speaks.
I am the land that listens, I am the land that broods;
Steeped in eternal beauty, crystalline waters and woods.

Long have I waited lonely, shunned as a thing accurst,
Monstrous, moody, pathetic, the last of the lands and the first;
Visioning camp-fires at twilight, and with a longing forlorn,
Feeling my womb o'er-pregnant with the seed of cities unborn.
Wild and wide are my borders, stern as death is my sway.
And I wait for the men who will win me—and I will not be won in a day;
And I will not be won by weaklings, subtle, suave and mild,
But by men with the hearts of vikings, and the simple faith of a child;
Desperate, strong and resistless, unthrottled by fear or defeat,
Them will I gild with my treasure, them will I glut with my meat.

"Lofty I stand from each sister land, patient and wearily wise,
With the weight of a world of sadness in my quiet, passionless eyes;
Dreaming alone of a people, dreaming alone of a day,
When men shall not rape my riches, and curse me and go away;
Making a bawd of my beauty, fouling the hand that gave—
Till I rise in my wrath and I sweep on their path and I stamp them into a grave.
Dreaming of men who will bless me, of women esteeming me good,
Of children born in my borders of radiant motherhood,
Of cities leaping to stature, of fame like a flag unfurled,
As I pour the tide of my riches in the eager lap of the world."

This is the Law of the Yukon, that only the Strong shall thrive;
That surely the Weak shall perish, and only the Fit survive.
Dissolute, damned and despairful, crippled and palsied and slain,
This is the Will of the Yukon,—Lo, how she makes it plain!

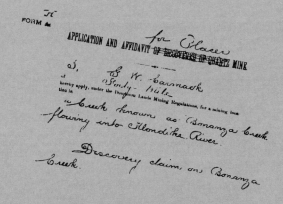

CHAPTER FOUR
GOLD

Discovery claim on Bonanza Creek in July 1898. It was
here in August 1896 that gold was first discovered,
sparking the greatest gold rush in world history. DM

An ingot of gold is being poured from the hot furnace in a gold refining room somewhere in Dawson, circa 1900. Ingots, or gold bars, were the easiest method of transporting raw gold to the outside. VPL

Over one-half million dollars in gold bricks at the Bank of British North America. AUTHOR'S COLLECTION

One and one-half tons of gold bricks and dust (in bags) inside the Alaska Commercial Company's store, June 1901.
UW, W&S

A distinguished-looking Chinese gentleman standing behind a large stack of gold dust sacks. DM

Gold being loaded on a stern-wheeler for the trip to Whitehorse. The 1899 gold shipment belonged to the Canadian Bank of Commerce.
DM, LARSS & DUCLOS

GOLD NUGGET BELT MADE FOR MISS ROSE BLUMKIN
BY ALBERT MAYER — LEADING JEWELER
DAWSON, Y. TER — PHOTO BY GOETZMAN.
— SEPT. 12, 99 —

CHAPTER FIVE

TRANSPORTATION

The Klondike Mines Railway ran 31 miles from Klondike City to Kings Dome. It started operations in 1906 to haul supplies and passengers to the dredge and hydraulic operations. Because of large losses, it went out of business in 1914. YA

A Klondike Mines Railway train crossing the Klondike River in winter. DM, C.H. CHAPMAN COLLECTION

A White Pass and Yukon Route winter stage arriving from Whitehorse loaded with passengers. In the early years this was the only regularly scheduled means of transportation between the two main population centers in the Yukon. White Pass ran this service as well as the steamers in the summer. The trip between the two towns could take five days or more, depending on weather conditions. The Administration Building is in the background.
UAA, CHARLES BUNNELL COLLECTION

TIME TABLE

Dawson Transfer Co.'s
STAGES

For Grand Forks,
4:00 p. m. Daily.

For Gold Bottom,
3:00 p. m. Daily.

TELEPHONE NO. 6

Office: N. C. Building, Dawson.

After the railroad was completed in 1900, the White Pass Railroad set up a stage route between Whitehorse and Dawson City. Wagons were used in the summer and sleds in the winter. The stage route did not follow the river except for a short distance from Carmacks to Minto, thus reducing the miles and time between the points. Airplanes took over most of the passenger and freight hauling in the winter by the early 1920s, and Dawson was opened to vehicular traffic in 1955. UW

An early 1900s view of two DeHaviland airplanes on a field near Dawson. Another form of earlier transportation—a dog team—was there to greet them.
DM, LOUISE BLACK COLLECTION

Two Fairchild 82, single engine aircraft tied up on floats on the Yukon River in Dawson, 1938. DM, HARBOTTLE COLLECTION

Two airplanes at Dawson. The airline was operated for quite a while by the White Pass and Yukon Route, which also ran the railroad to Whitehorse, the river steamers and the stage line. It was a total transportation company. The White Pass got into the airline business in 1934 and sold out to Yukon Southern Air Transport in 1941. In 1936, Ford Tri-motors, the most modern plane of the period, were purchased. They could carry 12 passengers and much cargo.
DM

Dan Coate's horse-drawn wagon literally bulging with mail sacks on Front Street outside the White Pass and Yukon Route freight shed along the waterfront.
UAA, BASSOC COLLECTION

Steam engine No. 3 destined for the Canadian Klondike Mining Company mine on Coal Creek is loaded on a wagon ready for transport, June 19, 1913. PAC, WOLFE PHOTO

A brewery wagon in front of the Klondike Brewery in Klondike City with engines of the Klondike Mines Railway in the background, early 1900s. There have been three known breweries in Dawson through the years.
DM, GEORGE ALAN JECKELL COLLECTION

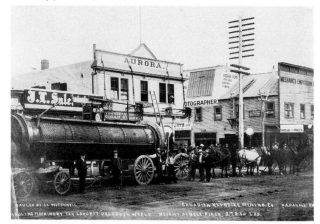

A drum for the world's largest dredge, owned by the Canadian Klondike Mining Company being hauled through Dawson. This single piece weighed 27,250 pounds.
DM, ADAMS PHOTO, DOROTHY WHYTE COLLECTION

Blitzen Bean was the holder of the Whitehorse to Dawson auto trip record in June 1913. No time was mentioned on the photo caption. DM, WOLFE PHOTO

The first automobile trip from Whitehorse to Dawson was probably a real adventure and was made in December 1912 when the wagon road was frozen. It took 33 hours to make the 365-mile trip. DM, DOODY

The bridge over the Klondike River that connected South Dawson and Klondike City, which was also known as Lousetown. The red light district, several businesses and a sawmill were located there. UAA, GOETZMAN, BASSOC COLLECTION

Opening of the Ogilvie Bridge over the Klondike River in April 1901. This bridge made access to the rich gold fields to the south easier. PAC

During the long winter months when the north country was frozen, some of the Yukon River steamers were stored at the Dawson slough, upriver from Dawson. This photo was taken during the winter of 1905-06.
YA, SCHARSCHMIDT COLLECTION

Before any bridges were built across the Klondike River, scows such as this were the only way across for men, supplies and animals on their way to Klondike City or the gold fields. DM

LEONARD INFLATING HIS BALOON, DAWSON JUNE 24. 1901.

CANTWELL

A large aerial balloon was inflated on Front Street in June
1901. VPL CANTWELL

Baseball was and still is a popular sport in Dawson. This is a July 4, 1903 game on the NWMP grounds.
DM, WOODSIDE

A baseball game, July 25, 1903.
UAA, TONI TROSETH
COLLECTION

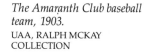

The Amaranth Club baseball team, 1903.
UAA, RALPH MCKAY
COLLECTION

The Colts Baseball Team, Yukon champions in 1904. DM

Ladies' Arctic basketball team. DM

Basketball was a sport that came to Dawson as soon as an adequate indoor facility was built. This is the Arctic Brotherhood's 1907 championship team. DM

The Arctic ski club. UW

Hockey was played anyplace a rink of ice could be cleaned off. This match in March 1900 matched local citizens against the police. The citizens won 8 to 0.
GA, GORDON CHANDLER COLLECTION

Hockey was a popular sport during the long Dawson winters. This is the Colts Hockey Team, Yukon champions in 1906 and 1907. DM, DOROTHY WHYTE COLLECTION

Curling was also popular during the long winter months. This group is the Dawson Ladies Curling Club in the 1920s. DM, ELLINGSEN

A lid was placed on top of the swimming pool of the Dawson Amateur Athletic Association in winter and ice was made for a circling rink. In 1978, years after the building was gone, old movies from the early 1900s were found in the swimming pool area, where they had been stored after the pool closed in 1931. The movies were frozen in the soil. DM

Tennis courts were built on land behind the Administration building early in the century, circa 1909. DM

Col. Hulme
H.E.A.Robertson
Jas. Hamilton Ro.
Harry Ridley
A.G. Smith
J.B. Patullo
Zack Woods
E.C. Senkler
Unknown
Frank McDougal
F.W. Gwillim (?)
R.W. Cautley
W.W. Cory
J.L. Coté
Nap. Harrison

Colley Devi.
G. White Fraser
Unknown
Mrs Crisp
Fred Crisp
Mrs C.C. Chalaway
O.S. Finnie
Fred Crisp
Mrs Duff Patrullo
H.G. Herbert
Mrs White-Fraser
Duff Patullo
C.S.W. Barwell
Mrs Zack Woods
Mrs Courtland Starnes
Mrs E.L. French
Mrs Ridley
Newton Storry
Mrs Wroughton
Mrs Arthur Davey
Mrs Colley-Davis
Unknown
Mrs F. McDougal
Mrs Congdon
Arthur Davey
F.T. Congdon
Billy White

Tennis Club at Dawson Y.T.
July. 1901.

There was a tennis club in Dawson as early as 1901. DM, FINNIE COLLECTION

D.A.A.A. Natatorium interior, 80,000 gallon capacity.
DM, ADAMS

Interior view of the Dawson Amateur Athletic Association Building. DM

Track meets were sometimes held on Front Street in early Dawson. Everyone in town must have turned out for this pole vaulting contest on July 4, 1899.
DM, HEGG, C.W. LINDEMANN COLLECTION

Residents of Dawson celebrating United States naval victories against Spain in 1898.
DM, NORVELL

A group of about 40 YOOP (Yukon Order of Pioneers) assembled for a photograph in the open park behind the Administration Building on Discovery Day 1925.
DM, HARBOTTLE COLLECTION

The Governor General of Canada, the Earl of Minto, visited Dawson in August 1900. Front Street was decked out with an elaborate archway and flags of both Canada and the United States. DM

A parade on Third Avenue, May 24, 1901. PAC

Discovery Day is celebrated every August 16 or 17. This is the parade on Front Street in 1935. DM, C. HAINES

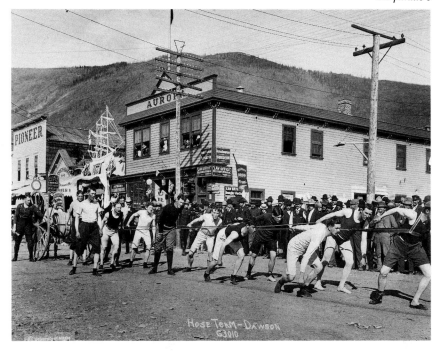

A hose team practicing the art of pulling the cart to a fire. This procedure resembles a dog team pulling a sled. Notice the sailing ship model on top of the building adjacent to the Aurora building. Perhaps it is advertising a steamship company or a display for a holiday or festival. UAA

Dawson, Y. T. Aug 5 1908

No. 6 **This is to Certify** that Dawson Lodge, No. 1, of the Independent Order of Odd Fellows, agrees to pay to Brother J. Ivan Seabrook or to any member of said order who is the holder of this certificate, the sum of Ten Dollars, $10.00, one year after date hereof, with interest at the rate of six per cent per annum, with the option to said Lodge to redeem this certificate at any earlier date upon payment of said Ten Dollars, $10.00, with interest to date of payment.

Trustees:
J. Seabrook
W. Pearce
F. Hickling

D. W. Ballantine
Noble Grand.
L. G. Bennet.
Secretary.

A truckload of Dawson citizens. The Dawson Hardware is still in business.
DM, HAZEL MCINTYRE COLLECTION

First masquerade ball for the benefit of the fire department given by the ladies of Dawson, Oct. 23, 1898.
UW, HEGG

A group portrait of the North American Transportation & Trading Company band and friends in front of the company's block on 1st Avenue, October 1899. PABC, LARRS & DUCLOS

AMUSEMENTS IN DAWSON CITY.

The library was decorated with Chinese parasols and lanterns for a tea party given in honor of the Governor General's visit. GA, GORDON CHANDLER COLLECTION

A pixie hatted, humorous artist at work in front of his shop on a sign advertising baths for gentlemen. VPL

Delivering water from a cart on King Street, 1900. VPL

Getting water from the Yukon River. PAC

CHAPTER SEVEN
WATERFRONT

ALONG THE WATER FRONT.

Steamer Columbian Sails With a Full Passenger List.

The floating dock and approach of the C. D. company was filled with people to bid good-bye to friends going out on the Columbian at 2 this afternoon. There were 100 passengers aboard, the sailing being enlivened by Messrs. Voorhees and Davis, playing "Home Sweet Home" on the banjo and guitar from the hurricane deck of the steamer.

Edward McGrath, a pioneer well known in Dawson, left accompanying his sister, Mrs. Rudolph, bound for Portland. His satchel contained fully $75,000 in gold dust, which he turned over to Purser Munro, for safe keeping. Among the other passengers were Ed Lewin, Ben Davis, Mr. and Mrs. John Boyle, Humboldt Gates, G. McPherren, Mrs. McKenny, Mr. and Mrs. B. Jeffry and Cad Wilson late of the Monte Carlo theater.

Steamer Flora left yesterday for White Horse with a fair list of passengers. This steamer has made the greatest number of round trips of any steamer on the river.

View of the Canadian, Columbian *and* Victorian *at the Dawson dock, 1899.* YA, WOODSIDE

-43-

*The Dawson waterfront in the summer of 1898 was a busy place with stampeders coming in from Lake **Bennett and St.** Michael, river boats bringing in supplies for the creeks and gold being shipped to the outside.* YA

Large group of spectators viewing a canoe race on the Yukon River, 1899. VPL

Scows landing at Dawson, 1898. The waterfront had built up considerably since the mass rush in the summer of 1897. UW

View of the Klondike Bridge spanning the Klondike River joining Klondike City to South Dawson. Men in canoes can be seen landing on shore, 1898.
DM, MCLENNAN COLLECTION

An early view of Klondike City, across the Klondike River from Dawson.
AUTHOR'S COLLECTION

A man in a pulley chair suspended high above the river on the wire running from the top of the ferry tower. The tower and other riverfront buildings, such as the present-day Canadian Bank of Commerce, are visible, 1900.
UAA, GOETZMAN, BASSOC COLLECTION

View looking north of the tower spanning Front Street. Other buildings, a stern-wheeler and the Klondike Mines Railroad tracks are also visible, 1904.
UAA, F.H. NOWELL, ERSKINE COLLECTION

The Hubrick Cable Ferry churning along on the Yukon River with Dawson in the background. The Ferry Tower is visible in the background as are the WP&YR docks and a sternwheeler, 1900.
VPL, ADAMS & LARKIN

The North West Mounted Police were the real heroes of the gold rush. While thousands of men streamed toward the gold fields, these men enforced the law, collected customs, and cared for the sick and destitute, while men around them were becoming millionaires. These men made the Yukon a safe place to live and work compared to the American camps. The first detachment of police arrived in the Yukon at Fortymile in 1894. It was reinforced after the rush started, until by 1900, the force numbered over 300 in the territory. YA, FAULKNER COLLECTION

CHAPTER EIGHT

NORTH WEST MOUNTED POLICE (RCMP)

Sam Steele was the commander of the North West Mounted Police in the North in 1898 and was called the "Lion of the Yukon" for his firm but honest rule of the gold rush. He enforced the order—which saved many lives—that every person entering the Yukon have a year's worth of supplies. He went on to become a general in World War I and a British knight. UW

North West Mounted Police Inspector, Charles Constantine. Constantine was born in England in 1849 and joined the NWMP in the 1880s. In 1895 he established a NWMP post at Fortymile, northwest of present-day Dawson and was on hand when the first gold find from the Klondike was recorded at Fortymile in 1896. Along with 20 constables, he established early law enforcement in the area and also acted as the mining recorder, coroner and a magistrate. He died in 1912. AMHA

Barracks and officers' cabins of the North West Mounted Police in Dawson. AMHA

THE KLONDIKE NUGGET.

VOL. 3 No. 21   DAWSON, Y. T., WEDNESDAY, SEPTEMBER 13, 1899   PRICE 25 CENTS

WRONG IS TRIUMPHANT

Colonel Steele Removed For No Cause.

STANDS IN THE WAY OF GOVERNMENT PETS.

Without Warning He Is Peremptorily Recalled.

A Man of Spotless Reputation Considered a Threat to Schemes and Schemers and Ordered Out of the Territory—Wrong Is Again Triumphant Upon the Yukon.

Colonel S. B. Steele, by long odds the most highly respected man on the Yukon today, has been peremptorily recalled to an obscure post of the Northwest Territory. The one competent and creditably honest official in Dawson has suffered the degradation of removal from a position he has honored and rendered most honorable, in a short incumbency of less than a year. The rapacious schemes of the Sifton gang of political pirates could not suffer the continuance of even one honest and competent member of an outlying government—a government constructed purely upon self interested lines and designed solely to acquiesce in the highhanded spoliation of a defenseless territory. Without one word of explanation, at a time when the merits of his man had won the confidence of every man, woman and child with the lapse of a year's experience on the Yukon...

equally the admiration and esteem of all with whom he came in contact. Of a stiff exterior and manner, but of sterling integrity, without so much as turning over a hand to win the appreciation of the press or public, without the slightest act which could have been construed as attempt to carry favor with influential people, of a gruff unapproachableness, the deposed commander of the N. W. M. P. has not only disarmed all criticism and all carping, but in eight months has won the laurels of public esteem to such a signal degree that his praises are resounding through the length and breadth of Canada and the United States and a thousand prospectors of every party and "ism" are pointing in unqualified approval to the one righteous man who, like Lot of old, has saved the Sodom and Gomorrah of Canadian officialism from the stigma of being utterly without excuse for further existence.

But the confiscation plans and concession programs of the gang temporarily in control of Canadian affairs caused them to look askance at the growing reputation of a man who was becoming famous for virtue, not for duplicity; for honesty and not for avariciousness; for temperance and not for...

Another Holdup.

About 9:30 o'clock last Sunday night, Mr. J. H. Johnson, proprietor of the Arlington restaurant, was held up by two masked men, near the Klondike bridge. The robbers stepped from the side of the road, directly in front of Johnson; one of them aimed a revolver at his head, and told him, in no uncertain tones, to throw up his hands; the other highwayman rifled Johnson's trousers pockets, relieving him of $250 in currency and a sack containing gold dust to the value of $150. No attempt was made to take his watch and chain, after securing the money and dust, the man holding the gun said: "Don't you try to move or yell, or I'll brain you where you are." Then both robbers ran towards the bridge. Johnson as soon...

LIEUTENANT-COLONEL S. B. STEELE.

SULPHUR DOING WELL.

Many Claims Join The Already Profitable Ones.

Steam Thawing—Steam Hoisting—Summer Sluicing and Extensive Preparations for Winter.

Sulphur creek claim owners are preparing for a heavy winter's work, and quite a number of claims were summer worked and pay located on several that were heretofore blanks.

The vicinity of the twenties below bear the marks of summer prospecting to a greater extent than any other portion of the creek. Last winter small pay was taken out near the creek, but on No. 18 good pay was located on the left, almost on the hillside, and the claims all lined up and struck the pay streak hard. Thirty-three below has been working a great portion of the summer and handling some very fine dirt.

Billy Strong, of 17 below, has some odd partnerships, but then Billy is not a bit stuck up over them. A negro woman and himself are the owners of a good Gold Run claim, and now the surveyors on Sulphur make the Queen a property holder and part owner of Billy's windlass, shaft and drift and right on the best of the pay. This fraction above 17 below is not the only one, and dozens have been lined out by Mr. Cautley and his surveyors, from ten to 200 feet. What a beautiful stampede would be on if the old law and ring were in vogue.

Eight below located the pay streak late in the spring and will work two steam thawers. Five and 4 below summer sluiced and will also be worked this winter. 3A and 3 were sold this spring and opened up in good shape by summer work. The claims are easily worked as the pay is in the creek bed.

That perseverance will win is shown on 12 above. Messrs. Moore and Hunter have prospected 12 above for two winters and took out a bare grub stake, yet they keep up spirits and this summer were rewarded by striking very fine pay some distance from the creek on the left. The first thousand buckets hoisted, and run down to the creek, sluiced 85 to the bucket and colors can be seen all through the dump. Mr. Moore will go outside, but Mr. Hunter will take out a dump and get the ground ready for extensive work next summer.

Twenty nine above was mostly drifted out last winter, and Slater brothers are just finishing the remainder with a thawer and the pay has been good.

Thirty-six above has the finest plant on the creek and one of the finest in the country. They have a double elevator and are tunneling and running the dirt on wheel barrows on the elevator and dump it in the sluice boxes.

Sulphur has very few hotels when compared with the other creeks. Sproull & Co. have started the McDonald hotel on 36 above and George Nunan has opened a road house on 3 below.

Maps of the Klondike and Stewart river districts for sale at the Nugget office.

ARCTIC SAW MILL

Come AND SEE OUR STOCK
It Will Pay You
The Ames Mercantile Co.

COURTESY STEPHEN GOLDMAN, PARKTON, MARYLAND

Looking across the Yukon River towards the front of the stockade of the N.W.M.P. Post. Tents pitched next to log stockade, boats pulled up on shore and men walking about, 1897. VPL

Bird's-eye view of the government reserve showing the R.C.M.P. police barracks square, left and the Administration building, center, 1919. GA, J.P. CLEMMITT COLLECTION

N.W.M.P. band, Dawson, 1901. PAC

Yukon Field Force.
ASL, GOETZMAN

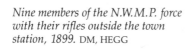

Nine members of the N.W.M.P. force with their rifles outside the town station, 1899. DM, HEGG

Detachment of the Yukon Field Force who "mushed" to Dawson in the winter of 1898-99. DM, HEGG

Christmas dinner, Yukon Field Force, 1899. The Maxim gun had an honored place in the dining room where it could be kept warm and was close to the parade ground. GA, ROY JOHNSTON COLLECTION

The Yukon Field Force drilling at Fort Herchmer in Dawson in 1900. The fort was built in 1897 by the North West Mounted Police for its headquarters. The Yukon Field Force was sent to Dawson to help the police maintain order in the predominantly American population and to prevent the Americans from possibly trying to annex the Yukon into the United States.
UW, LARSS & DUCLOS

Men of the Yukon Field Force drilling on the parade ground of the N.W.M.P. barracks. The Field Force was attached to the N.W.M.P. as an auxillary force, 1900.
DM, LARSS & DUCLOS

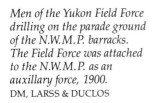

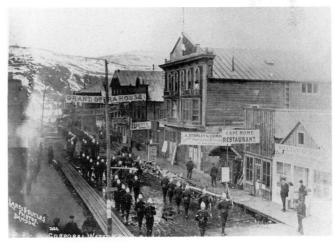

Yukon Field Force troops clad in their uniforms and pith helmets. AUTHOR'S COLLECTION

Dawson Rifles at Drill Hall, 1903. PAC

Seven Royal Canadian Mounted Police full dress uniform pose for a group photograph on the steps of the Administration Building in Dawson, 1930s. DM, MM COLLECTION

Monument to the Yukon Field Force placed in front of the steamer Keno.

CHAPTER NINE
STREET SCENES

A crowd waits for the mail in the summer of 1898. This log building was Dawson's fourth post office. UW, HEGG

The streets of Dawson were a
sea of mud after a rainstorm.
UW

A group of men and their
pack horses loaded with gear
and stoves on Front Street,
1898.
DM, MCLENNAN COLLECTION

First Avenue, 1890s.
GA, GORDON CHANDLER
COLLECTION

At the height of the gold rush (1897-99) the streets of Dawson were busy both day and night with the thousands of men and women who came looking for their "El Dorado." PARKS CANADA

Front Street had a number of buildings facing the river by 1898. PARKS CANADA

Street scene in early Dawson. The fire department kept in constant training because of the ever-present threat of fire. Dawson was a typical boom town—frame buildings and tents, boardwalks and muddy streets. One could almost sink out of sight in the streets after a heavy rain. YA, BETTS COLLECTION

Looking east along King Street. Offices of Dentists, Advocates, Real Estate agents, and a banner proclaiming the office of the 'Steamer Willie Irving,' are seen, 1900. VPL

First Avenue, north from Queen Street. This photo was taken at midnight on June 10, 1904.
AUTHOR'S COLLECTION

Second Avenue, south from King Street. This photo was also taken at midnight June 10, 1904.
AUTHOR'S COLLECTION

Front Street, 1908. AUTHOR'S COLLECTION

Post office and businesses on King Street. GA, ELLINGSEN

CHAPTER TEN
BUSINESSES

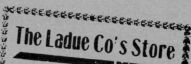

Foster, the sign painter, standing in front of his masterpiece, a large composite sign for advertising Dawson's leading businesses, 1900.
UAA, LARSS & DUCLOS, RALPH MCKAY COLLECTION

Gamblers pose at a table in Dawson. Gambling was the favorite pastime of the miners. Every form of gambling was in evidence and men would bet on anything. Stakes at the poker tables ran as high as $50,000 and many a casino changed hands on the flip of a card. AHL, GOETZMAN

Gold was worth $16 an ounce if clean, but if laced with black sand or brass filings brought far less. Gold dust from a miner's poke was weighed on gold scales and then exchanged for merchandise or services. As men became richer, price became immaterial; there was more gold than could be spent in a lifetime, or so people thought. UW, LARSS & DUCLOS

Exterior of one of H.W. Butler's Grocery stores. Palace Restaurant is next door. UW, GOETZMAN

Interior of H.W. Butler's grocery store. By 1903 Butler had two stores: on Queen Street and Third Avenue and on Albert Street and Second Avenue. UW, ADAMS

The Arctic Meat Company. AUTHOR'S COLLECTION

Interior of a store specializing in toiletries, early 1900s. DM

Interior of the dentist office of Dr. A.J. Gillis. He practiced medicine as well. His office was probably located in his residence. The dental chair, drill and related equipment, an open (roll top) desk, numerous books and magazines, print wall paper, a partial view of his diplomas, etc., are all visible. This was taken after 1902 but the exact date is unknown. YA, A.J. GILLIS

Interior view of Zaccarelli Book Store on King Street in the early 1900s. The store sold books, phonographs, post cards and related items. Zaccarelli's Pictorial Souvenir Book of the Golden Northland, published in 1908, left a great visual record of Dawson after the rush was over. AUTHOR'S COLLECTION

Exterior view of a log structure located on Bridge Street near the cliff. In front are employees watching a dog team pull a wooden cart (marked 'Eldorado Bottling Co.') filled with bottles, summer 1899. UW, BARLEY

Photo of merchandise and supplies piled on the Front Street wharf in Dawson. Businesses visible include: Arthur Lewin General Merchandise, 1898. YA, MCLENNAN COLLECTION

Avery's Grocery Store apparently offered a wide variety of grocery items. UAA

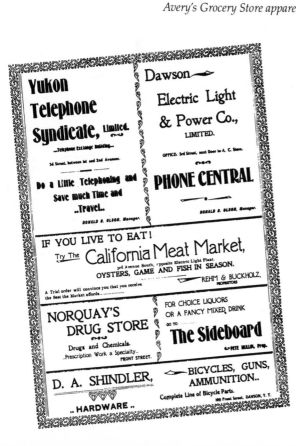

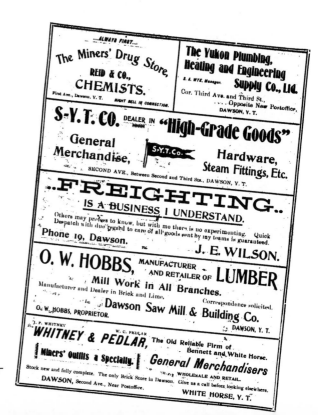

An early drug store. Notice that the buildings are actually log construction with false fronts built of clapboard and even tin siding, as with the building on the right. YA, BETTS COLLECITON

Klondike sawmill, Lousetown, 1899. GA, GORDON CHANDLER COLLECTION

A front view of the Dawson Daily News office on Third Avenue between King and Queen, 1915. This building is still standing. YA

Dawson Daily News staff on Oct. 7, 1899. The newspaper was published from 1899 through 1953.
UAA, RALPH MCKAY COLLECTION

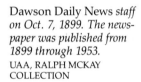

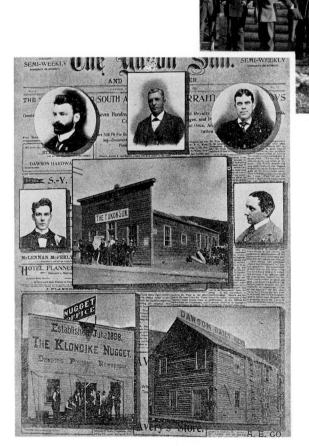

The semi-weekly, The Yukon Sun, *1900 edition with other Dawson newspaper buildings imposed on the photograph along with men presumably staff members of the* Sun.
AUTHOR'S COLLECTION

The Bank of British North America at the corner of Second Avenue and Queen Street won the race to Dawson in the summer of 1898 and did a thriving business for many years. The bank building today has been restored to its original look.
UW, ELLINGSEN

Shipment of $1 million in gold for the U.S. Mint. A wagon and group of approximately 19 men are shown outside the Canadian Bank of Commerce in Dawson with the boxes of gold, 1898.
DM, CANADIAN BANK OF COMMERCE COLLECTION

The first Canadian Bank of Commerce was housed in this log building. In 1899 the present building was built on the banks of the Yukon. Later tin siding was added for the look the building has now. YA

The Canadian Bank of Commerce, shown here, and the Bank of British North America raced each other to Dawson in 1898. The latter won, but both did a booming business shipping the gold outside. Paper money was exchanged for the gold dust as it was less cumbersome to handle. YA, WOODSIDE

The Alaska Exploration Company building, 1899. This building later became the headquarters for the Northern Commercial Company. GA, GORDON CHANDLER COLLECTION

Staff of the Northern Commercial Company in 1901.

The Northern Commercial Company on the corner of First and King Street, 1908. DM

One of the earliest trading companies in the area was the Alaska Commercial Company based in San Francisco and founded years before the gold rush. The company merged with the Alaska Exploration Company in 1901. Later taken over by the Northern Commercial Company. DM

The North American Trading and Transportation Company's building in 1897. The company was founded by John Healy from Dyea in the 1880s, backed by the Cudahy family meat-packing fortune. The business closed in 1912. AMHA

Float of the Alaska Commercial Company, "We were here first," in front of the A.C. Co. building. Part of Victoria Day celebrations, May 24, 1901. UW, GOETZMAN

Interior of the Dawson cafe, 1902.
DM, CARREL COLLECTION

Arcade Cafe
Harry Gleaves, Prop.
Dawson, Yukon Territory, Canada
DISCOVERY DAY, AUGUST 17, 1936

MENU

SOUP

Rice Tomato, a la Collins   Chicken Consomme, a la Pinska

FISH

Fresh-Caught King Salmon Fishwheel Fry .... $ .75

BOILED

Pelly River Chicken, Bonanza Nuggets 1.00

ENTREES

Baby Moose Steak, Whisky Hill Grill .... .75
Eldorado Caribou Cutlets, Last Chance Jelly .... .75
Pork Sausage and Mashed Potatoes, Nigger Jim's Favorite .... .75
Combination Cold Lunch, Iceworm Salad .... .75
Sirloin Steak, Cheechako's Delight 1.00
T-Bone Steak, Fairbanks Special 1.25
Lamb Chops, a la Bob Service Grill 1.00

ROASTS

Stuffed Tom Turkey, Trail of '98 .... 1.50
Leg of Pork, Diamond Tooth Gertie Apple Sauce 1.00
Prime Ribs of Beef, Klondike Kate's Delight 1.00
Milk-Fed Chicken, Husky Dressing, Lone Star Roast 1.25

COLD MEATS

Young Chicken and Pure Gold Salad 1.00

VEGETABLES

Yukon-Grown Steamed and Mashed Potatoes
Garden Island Combination Vegetables

SALADS

Combination Salad, Matanuska Dressing 1.00
Sliced Tomatoes and Cucumbers, Anchorage Dressing .... .75

DESSERT

Ridgetop Pumpkin Pie .... .25 Fresh Glacier Apple Pie .... .25
Frozen North Five-Egg Custard Pie, .25

EXTRAS

Chicken Tamales .... .75 Chili Con Carne .... .25
Tomato Soup .... .50 Fresh Cow's Milk .... .25
Asparagus Tips, with Skookum Jim Mayonnaise, 1.00
Northern Lights Tea—Bear Creek Ice Water—Midnight Dome Coffee
THE LAND OF SUNSHINE AND PURE GOLD

Arcade Cafe
Harry Gleaves, Prop.
AUGUST, 31 1940 Dawson, Yukon Territory, Canada   SATURDAY.

PINEAPPLE JUICE, 25	GRAPE FRUIT.....25
ORANGE JUICE.....25 MENU	APPLE SAUCE.....25
STEWED PRUNES, 25	STEWED APRICOTS, 25
FRESH BLUEBERRIES,25	APPLE JUICE.....25

SOUP.
RICE TOMATO SOUP.

FISH. -
STEAMED FINNAN HADDIE, FRESH CAUGHT WHITEFISH, 75
CANNED SALMON POTATO SALAD................75

-BOILED-
ALL YUKON VEGETABLE DINNER.................76

-ENTREES-
BEEF STEW AND FRESH YUKON VEGETABLES..75
BREADED FRESH CARIBOU CUTLETS & JELLY...75
FRESH KILLED MOOSE STEAK, TENDER & JUICY. 75
ASSORTED MEATS WITH POTATO SALAD..........75
HAMBURGER STEAK & FRIED ONIONS..............75
FRIED HOME MADE PORK SAUSAGE...............75
OMELETTES, JELLY, HAM, CHEESE, ,,,,,,,,,75
MINCED HAM WITH SCRAMBLED EGGS...........75
LOIN FRESH KILLED PORK CHOPS.............1.00
SIRLOIN STEAK FRIED POTATOES.............1.00

-ROASTS.-
MILK FED CHICKEN & DRESSING...........1.00
PRIME RIB OF BEEF AU JUS.............1.00
LEG OF PORK APPLE SAUCE...............75
LEG OF FRESH KILLED MOOSE APPLE JELLY,75

-DESSERT-
CHOCOLATE BLANC MANGE, PRUNES, APPLE SAUCE.
ICE CREAM, APPLE OR RAISIN PIE. ....

-EXTRAS-
CINNAMON ROLLS, CUP CAKES.25 COOKIES......25
MILK SHAKES 25, COCA-COLA, FRESH MILK.....25
ICE CREAM SUNDAES,25, TOMATO, SALMON SAN. 25
DENVER SANDWICH ON TOAST, 50, TOMATO SOUP...50
OYSTER STEW- 75, CHILI CON CARNE, 75 MILK TOAST.

D.W. Ballentine's garage located on Third Avenue. The first car was brought to Dawson on the steamer, Whitehorse, *on July 11, 1907.* GA, ELLINGSEN

The Empire Hotel located on the north side of Queen Street just west of Second Avenue, 1900. YA

At the height of the rush you could buy almost anything in Dawson from the finest Paris fashions to the best champagne to freshly killed game. Anything was for sale for enough gold. If you did not strike it rich on the creeks but had good luck and fortitude, you might make a fortune as a merchant, showman or bar owner. Some of the richest men went south with money made on the streets of Dawson rather than on the creeks. The streets were paved with gold if you knew how to mine them. AHL, GOETZMAN

CHAPTER ELEVEN
BUILDINGS

A Carnegie Library was built in 1904 and was to be the envy of many other towns for years. It remained open until 1924 when the building was nearly destroyed by fire. Taken over by the Yukon Lodge #45 A.F.&A.M. in 1934. YA, CHISHOLM

St. Andrew's Presbyterian Church on the south side of Church Street in 1903. It was built in 1901 by Robert Moncrief, under the supervision of Reverend Andrew S. Grant, to replace the original small log church which burned in 1898. At the time it was the only church with regulation pews and an organ which was operated by a water motor in the basement. The manse behind the church, which has been restored by Parks Canada, was also built in 1901. The Good Samaritan Hospital was at one time on a lot adjoining the church. The church was closed in 1932.
PAC, WOODSIDE

Interior view of St. Andrew's Church.
AUTHOR'S COLLECTION

Interior of the first St. Mary's Catholic Church located at the north end of Front Street.
GA, GORDON CHANDLER COLLECTION

Partial panorama of private homes and cabins along the hillside in north Dawson near 'Nob Hill,' where the 400 resided, 1900. UAA GOETZMAN

The government telegraph office was designed by government architect, Thomas W. Fuller, in July 1899. He arrived in Dawson in July 1899 and designed most of the government buildings, most of which are still standing. He went on to become the Chief Architect of Canada, a position his father once held. DM, FULLER COLLECTION

Proposed Recording Office & Administration Blg.
DAWSON, Y. T.

FRONT ELEVATION

Drawing by T.W. Fuller.
PUBLIC ARCHIVES CANADA
PUBLIC RECORDS DIV., RG. 11.

This building was the one government building to be continually occupied since construction. It is with pride that locals note that from 1901-1953 it was the center of federal and territorial government activities in the Yukon and from 1924 to 1961 the only active government building in Dawson. A total of 12 of the Yukon's commissioner's had their offices here. The first territorial council with any elective representation at all converged while the building was under construction and the first wholly elective council sat here in 1908. The Dawson Council and the Territory Council all sat here. It has, for a period housed all the federal departments operating in the Yukon before 1953. It has seen long public service as a post office, telegraph office, school and radio station. The building was restored by the Yukon government and rededicated in 1986. It now houses the Dawson Museum as well as offices in various government departments and the Territorial Council holds regular sessions here. DM & VPL

The Dawson Amateur
Athletic Association building
was the center of the city's
recreational activities.
Through the years it served
as a gym, hockey arena,
swimming pool and theater.
The building was destroyed
by fire in 1938.
YA, FINNE COLLECTION

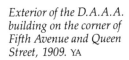

Yukon grown vegetables
displayed at the Yukon Fair in
the D.A.A.A. building,
1908. AUTHOR'S COLLECTION

Exterior of the D.A.A.A.
building on the corner of
Fifth Avenue and Queen
Street, 1909. YA

The Commissioner's residence was built in 1901 and designed by T.W. Fuller to provide a permanent residence. The first resident was Commissioner James Ross. The house cost $42,000 and had electricity, hot air heat, and an elegant ginger-bread appearance outside. Inside plumbing was added in 1903. It was rebuilt in 1908 after the disastrous fire, to its present less-austere appear-ance. The last commissioner to occupy the house was George Black who left for military service in 1916. This view was taken in August 1906. UAA

A fire on Dec. 26, 1906, badly damaged the residence.
YA, BETTS COLLECTION

Interior view of the residence.
AUTHOR'S COLLECTION

The Arctic Brotherhood Hall, was built in October 1901. It was purchased in 1930 by the Fraternal Order of Eagles. Sold privately in 1942. Charles Butchard later sold "shares" to local residents to preserve the building and prevent it from being demolished and sent to whitehorse. The city acquired it around 1950 and it was restored in 1967 as the community's centennial project. It is leased to K.O.A. for Diamond Tooth Gertie's and other community events. It was restored in 1983. YA

Interior of Arctic Brotherhood Hall on Fourth Avenue. Decorated for the 10th Anniversary of the founding of the Fraternal Order of Eagles, Dawson Aerie No. 50, Feb. 6, 1908. PABC, LARSS & DUCLOS

The impressive public school building, designed by T.W. Fuller, was opened in 1901. The building was destroyed by fire by 1956.
DM & UAA ELLINGSEN

Discovery Day in front of the public school, 1918.
AUTHOR'S COLLECTION

Designed by Thomas W. Fuller, this building was completed in November 1900 and housed the Post Office, Customs Office, Telegraph Office, Crown Land Office and Registrar's Office. This was Dawson's sixth Post Office in less than four years. The previous five locations had all been of a temporary nature due to the failure of the Federal Post Office Department to believe that the gold rush would be anything but a flash in the pan and so considered an organized and efficient mail service a ridiculous waste of time. When the Government called for tenders for the construction of the impressive edifice, many local contractors placed a bid. Ottawa was staggered by the exceedingly high bids received from Dawson contractors although these were moderate bids by local standards. Government officials were not willing to pay these inflated prices so imported a government construction crew from Atlin, B.C. to work under architect Fuller's supervision who, himself, was swinging a hammer to meet the completion deadline. The Post Office building was the first substantial public building completed in Dawson and was the pride of Dawsonites. It closed in 1923.

The money order department. UAA, CANTWELL

Waiting to get their mail.
PARKS CANADA

NEW COURT HOUSE DAWSON.Y.T. ADAMS&LARKIN PHOTO.

One of six buildings designed by Thomas W. Fuller, the Court House was completed in 1901. With population decline and consolidation of government administration space, the Court was moved to the Administration Building. The Court House was then used only intermittently until 1950 when the Sisters of St. Ann transferred their hospital to this building after St. Mary's Hospital was destroyed by fire. They continued to run the hospital until 1963 when the Territorial Government took over the administration. It is now Parks Canada Administration Office.

A murder trial in June 1901 at the new courthouse. PAC, WOODSIDE

$10,000 IMPROVEMENTS

Extensive Improvements Being Made to St. Mary's Hospital.

St. Mary's hospital is undergoing extensive improvements and additions. An addition is being made to the west wing. the front of the building that will add 20 feet to the width. The roof will be extended so as to include the addition. the whole front will be faced up with planed lumber. giving to the building the handsome front of 40 feet. the wing extending back that width for 50 feet. The new addition will be devoted to private wards. and this will give this whole extensive wing to that purpose. In this wing also there will be a new operating room with skylights and fitted with every essential of such a room in a modern hospital. There will altogether be 150 beds in the hospital when the improvements are completed and 15 private rooms. Several bath rooms have also been fitted up with hot and cold water. The improvements now being made will represent an expenditure of $10,000. but when completed St. Mary's will be in the list of first class hospitals.

CHAPTER TWELVE
HOSPITALS

St. Mary's Hospital at the upper end of Dawson. DM

Father Judge seated under a canvas-covered shelter equipped with benches and a stove in Dawson. St. Mary's Hospital is under construction in the background. Only part of the log wall is up and the window frames are in, June 1897. Father William Judge came to Dawson from Fortymile in the winter of 1896-97. He opened a church and hospital and treated the many sick of Dawson until his untimely death in January 1899. He was very well-respected and became known after his death as "the Saint of Dawson." ASL

St. Mary's Hospital and Roman Catholic Church. DM

A panorama of Dawson from the edge of the Dome above St. Mary's Hospital, 1930s. DM, C. TIDD

St. Mary's Hospital taken from a military flight over Dawson during World War II. The church was torn down by this time. The hospital was destroyed by fire in 1951.
RANDY ACCORD, FAIRBANKS, ALASKA

Interior of the ward in the Good Samaritan Hospital with patients in their beds, two nurses, two orderlies and two doctors standing and seated around a table and stove in the center of the ward, 1900. The hospital was the second to be built in Dawson, in August 1898. It was partially funded by the Canadian government.
YA, LARSS & DUCLOS

The spread of disease was a constant problem in Dawson since the town was built on a swampy area and proper sanitary conditions were practically nonexistent. This is a smallpox hospital in 1899 which was apparently placed far from the city limits.
ASL, CHARLES BUNNELL COLLECTION

PUBLIC NOTICE.

The public are warned that cases of typhoid fever have during the past two seasons been reported from the following points:

ON BONANZA CREEK.

No. 76 below discovery.
No. 60 below discovery.
King Solomon's hill.
Oro Fino hill.
Magnet village.
No. 11 below discovery.
No. 7 below discovery.
The town of Bonanza.
No. 3 above discovery.
No. 26 above discovery.

ON GOLD RUN.

No. 12B.	No. 13.
No. 25.	No. 47.
No. 27.	No. 50.
No. 42.	

ON ELDORADO.

No. 12 Eldorado.
No. 17 Eldorado.

ON HUNKER.

At Gold Bottom.

ON SULPHUR.

No. 2 below discovery.
No. 36 below discovery.

ON DOMINION.

No. 7 below lower discovery.
No. 235 below lower discovery.
No. 241 below lower discovery.
No. 243 below lower discovery.
At Granville.

As typhoid fever is generally contracted from drinking water polluted by the excreta of typhoid patients, residents of the creeks in the above localities are particularly warned to secure the water they use for drinking and domestic purposes from an unpolluted source. All water in the above mentioned localities used for drinking (no matter from what source secured) should be boiled for at least twenty minutes to ensure thorough sterilization, and then cooled. This precaution of boiling the drinking water ought to be observed at all points where there is any suspected danger of contamination from privies.

To lessen the danger of future infection the public are hereby warned to observe the following precautionary measures respecting water supply, privies, disposal of excreta, garbage, etc.

WATER SUPPLY.

Water for drinking, cooking and other domestic use should be taken from

(a) Genuine springs (uncontaminated) ; (well cribbed and protected) ;
(b) Glaciers (pure) ;
(c) Snow (clean) ;
(d) Rain water off clean or metal roofs, but should be boiled for drinking ;
(e) Gulches on which there are no habitations or mining operations, but if vegetable contamination is suspected, the water used for drinking should be boiled ; or
(f) Wells at least fifty feet distant from the creeks or the Klondike, and 100 feet distant from privies on the same or a lower level.

Water for drinking and domestic use should not be taken from

(a) Any main creek such as Bonanza, Eldorado, Hunker, Dominion, Sulphur, Gold Run, or from any tributaries which are being worked or on which there are dwellings ;
(b) Old shafts or prospect holes. (Two cases of typhoid fever occurred on Oro Fino hill through the patients drinking water from an abandoned shaft there.)
(c) Ice taken from open cuts in the creek valley into which the creek water is in danger of seeping.

PRIVIES.

Privies should be provided with water tight boxes to be used as receptacles for the excreta. They should, in summer, be placed at least thirty feet from any dwelling ; and in winter they may be placed nearer if emptied very frequently or provided with special apparatus for carrying off any malodor or impurity. A small quantity of ashes or earth should be emptied daily into the boxes.

During the summer (1st of May to 1st of November) these privy boxes should be emptied weekly and at a distance of at least 300 yards from any dwelling, and the contents when dry burned.

No privy should be allowed to become offensive at any time.

No privy should be placed over a creek or gulch, nor should any excreta or garbage be thrown into the creek or gulch.

Privies having deep pits beneath them should be placed at least 100 feet from any dwelling. When filled within one foot of the surface the building should be moved over a new pit, and the remaining portion of the old pit filled with earth. This class of privy, however, is not recommended.

HOUSE AND STABLE REFUSE.

Between May 1st and November 1st all solid household refuse, decaying vegetable or animal matter or other rubbish should be placed in a suitable receptacle and dumped once or twice weekly into heaps at a distance of a hundred yards from any dwelling and burned when dry. Liquid refuse should be emptied into separate receptacles and emptied twice a week at a distance of at least 100 yards from any dwelling and at such places as not to contaminate any water supply.

The cans after being emptied should be thrown on a dump with the solid garbage, excreta and refuse, so that the vegetable and animal contents still adhering to them may be destroyed when the heap is burned.

Foul water should not be allowed to accumulate on or near any premises.

No stable should be placed nearer than a hundred feet to a dwelling. Stable yards should be cleaned once a month during the season from May 1st to November 1st. No stables or yards should be allowed to become offensive at any time.

J. N. E. BROWN,
Territorial Health Officer.

CHAPTER THIRTEEN

ENTERTAINMENT AND THE PALACE GRAND THEATER

The Palace Grand Theater on King Street, restored in 1967.

Entertainment and the Palace Grand Theater

▼

The Palace Grand was not the first theater to be built in the district. Even before gold was discovered at Bonanza in 1896, small canvas-covered or wood-frame shanty theaters had existed in placed like Circle City and Fortymile. These humble structures, usually a combination theater, dance hall and saloon, attracted miners from hundreds of miles away. From the outside these buildings all attempted to project an elegance which belied the dilapidated conditions of the interior. Cornices and pillars supporting fake balconies and ornate balustrades might form the two-story facade for a very small, poorly ventilated, canvas-roofed shack. The building would more than likely be divided into two rooms, the first containing a saloon and the second a combination theater-dance hall with a small stage at one end. Later, more solid two-story affairs were constructed which boasted a row of "private" boxes on the second floor. These compartments represented special status for the successful miner. Rented for an evening, he demonstrated to everyone "in the jostling, sweaty mob below" that he was a man of some substance and influence.

Performance in this early period could only be described as dreadful. There was little or no attempt at scenery and actors and actresses were generally of the lowest caliber. At the conclusion of the show the benches in front of the stage would be removed and a dance begun which might last till dawn the next day. The women, usually overweight, plain and on the "shady side of 30" went by such colorful aliases as Ethel the Moose, Mollie Fewclothes, Ping Pong, Moosehide Kate and Sweetie the Pig. Miners would pay for dances and then be coaxed into private boxes where they were expected to keep themselves and their escorts well-supplied with cheap, watered-down champagne. While the music continued unabated throughout the night, the men danced and drank, eventually stumbling to their rooms in the painful light of morning. In this early period theaters were few and far between and offered little more than conversation and a warm place to relax. To one observer, the women were "beauties all" but to another they were "pretty terrible compared with any ordinary woman back home." Of course, any woman who could put up with the privations of a northern existence in those days, would have possessed a somewhat robust constitution. The liquor was also inferior, consisting of cheap adulterated whiskey usually manufactured on the premises from a concoction of fusel oil. "Champagne" was heavily watered and sold for exorbitant prices.

Before the great rush, Dawson was essentially a city of tents and shacks, many of which were small saloons and gambling houses. Although some of these canvas buildings were actually small theaters, the first permanent wood theater in Dawson was a log building called the Opera House. It followed the essential pattern of the northern saloon-playhouse; a bar and gambling room in the front with a theater-dance hall behind. A row of private boxes were located on the second floor. The theater was actually quite small and could accommodate probably no more than 80 to 100 people. Candles served as footlights for the tiny stage while rough benches were placed in rows over the canvas-covered floor. The Pavillion theater opened in June 1898, advertised its production as featuring "first-class artists only." The Combination (later Tivoli) theater opened its doors in August proclaiming, "the finest formed women in the Klondike," while the Monte Carlo, which announced its grand opening on Aug. 6, stated that a "grand ball [would take place] after the performance." The ownership of theaters tended to change hands on a regular basis, consequently it was not unusual to see each establishment have two or three "grand openings" in a single year. Two new houses, the Novelty and Amphitheater, opened in the spring of 1899.

Except for the storehouses of the Northern Commercial and N.A.T.&T. companies, theaters were generally the largest buildings in town. Constructed almost entirely of wood, they were erected by workmen who sometimes toiled around the clock. The earlier use of tallow candles for lighting purposes soon gave way to gas chandeliers and candelabra, as well as primitive electric lights. Bars, which at one time had been only rough wood counters, were now of polished oak or pine and fronted large, elegant, glass mirrors. Furniture, too, became more decorative as the theaters and dance halls became increasingly popular.

The variety and quality of the shows was also improved. As word of the riches of the Klondike spread over the world, more and more theatrical entrepreneurs, drama companies and vaudeville acts made their way to the Yukon alongside the gold hungry miners. Dawson was now included in the circuit of many companies who traditionally traveled up and down the west coast. Performances became more professional and changed with amazing rapidity.

Greater diversification was demanded by men who perhaps only a few months before had been living in New York or San Francisco. The poor quality of shows, which had satisfied the old sourdoughs prior to 1898, were no longer tolerated by the young cheechakos. Actresses and dance hall girls tended to be younger, prettier, and more accomplished, with very few doubling as prostitutes.

Theater-dance halls in Dawson, by the summer of 1899, were one of the most prosperous service industries of the gold rush. For those who had capital enough to erect a building and bring in performers, sizable profits could be made. The town was open. Gambling and drinking flourished under few restrictions and theaters were packed almost every night. Dawson was full of men, pouches of gold dust in hand, who were in from the creeks and ready to "tie one on." As well, new arrivals from the south enjoyed the night life before getting down to the business of filing claims. Some, of course, never left. The Dawson theater and dance hall capitalized upon the whims of men who, after trekking thousands of miles to the goldfields, spent their earnings in wild sprees. Normally sober individuals, when placed in the frenzied atmosphere of Dawson, were capable of gambling away thousands of dollars in a couple of minutes, or spending small fortunes on numerous rounds of champagne. As Diamond Tooth Gertie summed it up, it was as if "the poor ginks just have to spend it, they're so scared they'll die before they can get it out of the ground."

The need for a larger, more lavish playhouse in Dawson became apparent by the spring of 1899. The Palace Grand (or as it was originally called, the Grand Opera House) fulfilled this need, being large enough to stage major productions and seat 600 to 700 people. It proved to be the most elegant theater in town. The architecture, both inside and out, was more ornate than any playhouse before it, and the Palace Grand soon epitomized the growth of entertainment in Dawson. Its history is in many ways the history of theater in the Klondike.

The Palace Grand Theater
▼

When the Grand Opera House opened in July 1899, it was billed as the biggest and best theater north of San Francisco and west of Winnipeg. On opening night Dawson turned out

in force and although some of the paint was still wet and several stray malamutes had to be ejected, the evening was a great success. For the next few months a wide variety of acts graced its stage and whenever the other entertainment failed, Arizona Charlie would mount the stage in his fringed buckskins and give a demonstration of his marksmanship by shooting glass balls from between the fingers of his wife. One night he shot her finger off—she insisted they drop the act.

In October 1899, "The Grand" became "The Palace Grand." A year later it was renamed the "Savoy" and later still, "the Old Savoy." During this period various owners changed the layout—the lobby lost the bar and gained a shooting gallery, among other things. The theater finally became The Auditorium and during the early 1900s saw everything from legitimate theater to bazaars and dances. In the late '30s it was called the Klondike Nugget Dance Hall, but whatever its name, the old building continued to entertain thousands until 1940 when it was closed.

Reconstruction of the theater began in 1960, under the direction of the Federal Department of Northern Affairs and National Resources, and because the structure was in such poor condition, restoration was not possible. When Meadows built the theater, he was unaware of the effects of permafrost. Over the years, the building shifted so much and the wood rotted to such an extent that by 1960 it was no longer safe for public use.

After careful study of each detail and feature of the building, the structure was dismantled piece by piece and a replica of the original 1899 building was reconstructed. Samples of wallpaper, hardware, lighting features and interior furnishings were taken from the old building and duplicated to be installed in the new theater. In 1962, the new Palace Grand theater was officially opened to the public.

Today the theater is owned by the Canadian Parks Service and each summer is leased to the Klondike Visitors Association for the "Gaslight Follies" show. In addition, Parks Canada guides offer tours of the facilities daily throughout the summer.

COURTESY LINDA BIERLMEIER, CANADIAN PARKS SERVICE, KLONDIKE NATIONAL HISTORIC SITES

Arizona Charlie Meadows

Charles Henson Meadows, or as he was commonly known, "Arizona Charlie Meadows," was one of the gold rush's best known characters.

He was born on March 10, 1860 in Visalia, Calif. to parents who had come west a few years before by wagon train. Charlie learned to master the lariat and horses as a young man on the Tulure County plains. The Meadows family moved their stock and possessions to the Tonto Basin in Arizona when Charlie was 16.

His father and two brothers were killed in a fight against a group of Apache Indians in 1882 and Meadows became a dedicated Indian fighter. In the following years he became a World's Champion cowboy and lassoist. His fame led him to be asked to join a circus wild west show leaving for Australia. He performed with the Wirth Brothers show and several others throughout Southeast Asia before joining Buffalo Bill's Wild West Show in England. In 1893 he founded his own show, "Arizona Charlie's Historical Wild West," and toured the United States and Mexico.

The lure of the Klondike was made for Meadow's adventuresome spirit, and with 12 other men and seven tons of provisions he crossed the Chilkoot Pass in 1897. His party suffered many misfortunes along the way including a boat wreck, losing their outfit in a Sheep Camp flood, having their horses die from eating poison grass, and being frozen in at Stewart River before reaching Dawson.

After landing in Dawson, Meadows wasted little time buying controlling interest in some gold mines. He also purchased *The Klondike News* shortly after arriving in town but soon sold it for a large profit.

With his new wealth he decided to build the grandest theater in town—he couldn't get his love for show business out of his system.

On July 18, 1899, Meadows opened his theater, the Grand Opera House, to a large crowd and acted as the master of ceremonies, appearing in his familiar buckskin jacket and Mexican sombrero.

Charlie was a large man, six foot six, and very handsome. He was married twice, first on the high seas off the coast of the Philippines and the second time just before leaving for the Klondike.

At his new theater, when people in the audience appeared bored, Meadows would treat them to displays of his shooting skills. Dressed in his usual buckskin and sombrero with his long black locks hanging below his shoulders, he would shoot cigarettes from his wife's mouth and glass balls from between her fingers. On one occasion, Charlie accidentally removed the tip of his wife's thumb with an errant shot.

Meadows gave up management of the theater in October 1899 but kept the bar and saloon that were in the building. During the next two years the theater had many difficulties, some relating to management and some to the fact that the gold rush was waning and a new rush had begun for Nome, Alaska in 1900. The theater's name was changed from the Grand Opera House to the Palace Grand Theater, then the Savoy and finally to the Old Savoy, but business slumped and Meadows sold his interest in October 1901.

Besides his Yukon adventure, Meadows' exciting life included bullfighting in Mexico, leading a party of invaders to a cannibal island and fighting the broadsword champion of the world. Eventually he settled on a ranch near Yuma, Ariz., where he died at the age of 72 on December 9, 1932. He is buried in Yuma.

World-famous cowboy and showman "Arizona Charlie Meadows." JEAN KING, GRANADA HILLS, CA.

GREAT MEXICAN BULL FIGHT
FIESTA AND EQUESTRIAN CARNIVAL.

Cripple Creek, Colo., August 24, 25 and 26.

1895

CAVLOS GARCIA

THE WORLD'S MOST FAMOS BULL FIGHTER,

AND

I Full Troop of MATADORS.

Over $5,000 in Mexican Costums

LA CHARRITTA

THE ONLY LADY BULL FIGHTER IN THE WORLD.

A Carload of Cazadero Bulls

Direct from the famous Cazadero Ranch in Mexico.

Bred for fighting purposes only.

"ARIZONA CHARLEY."

The King of Cowboys America's Champion all-round Shot, and the only living man who performs the difficult feat of shooting flying targets from a running horse with both pistol and rifle. Exhibited before all the crowned heads of the old world. The winner in one hundred cowboy tournaments and contests.

KING OF COWBOYS

ARIZONA CHARLIE

ARIZONA CHARLIES'
EQUESTRIAN CO.

Late from a triumphant tour of the world.

KID MEADOWS
Champion Rider

MISS ROSE HIGGINS,
Queen Equestrienne of California.

MISS MAE MELBOURNE,

MISS ALICE HAMILTON.

BULL FIGHT OR MONEY RETURNED.

BOX OF SIX SEATS
SINGLE SEAT IN BOX
FIRST CLASS SEAT
SECOND CLASS SEAT

J. H. WOLFE, Manager

-91-

Arizona Charlie Meadows at the opening of his magnificent theater on July 18, 1899. UW

Grave marker at Yuma, Ariz.

The "Arizona Charlie's Hotel, Casino, Bingo and Bowling," complete with a facade of the Palace Grand Theater in Dawson, was opened on South Decatur Boulevard in Las Vegas, Nevada in April 1988.

COURTESY JEAN KING, GRANADA HILLS, CALIFORNIA

The showplace of Dawson, The Palace Grand Theater, possibly at the time of its opening in July 1899. UW, LALRSS & DUCLOS

Looking west on the north side of King Street with the Palace Grand in the center, 1899. PABC, LARSS & DUCLOS

Scenes of the 1898 and 1899, St. Andrew's Day ball at the Palace Grand. The celebration, held on Nov. 30, commemorates the martyrdom in about 70 A.D. of Saint Andrew, patron saint of Scotland. Saint Andrew was the brother of Saint Peter and one of the 12 Apostles of Christ, and many branches of the Christian Church celebrate November 30 as his feast day. DM, LARSS & DUCLOS AND YA

Many plays were held in the Palace Grand (called the Auditorium in this 1907 photo). Here the actors pose on the set of "Captain Swift." DM

This is the supper scene from the first act of "Camille" by the Lillian M. Hall Stock Company players. The photo dates from 1903.
DM, ADAMS & LARKIN

Professor Freimuth's 11-piece orchestra in formal attire poses for a group picture in front of a classical backdrop on the stage of the Palace Grand. No date. DM

By the 1950s, the "Palace Grand," later called the "Savoy," the "Old Savoy," and "The Auditorium" was run down. These people are members of the Klondike Tourist Bureau (forerunner of K.V.A.) who produced "The Shooting of Dan McGraw" in the 1950s. DM

COLLISEUM THEATRE
DAWSON CITY, YUKON

Names of the theatre through the years:

July 1899-October 1899
Grand Opera Theater
Oct. 1899-Aug. 1900
Palace Grand Theater
Aug. 1900-Sept. 1901
The Savoy
Nov. 1901-1938
Auditorium
1938-1940
Nugget Dance Hall
1940-1962
Auditorium
July 1, 1962-present
Palace Grand Theater

The theater building had deteriorated so much by 1940 that it was closed, thus ending 41 years of use. The condition was so bad that when Parks Canada examined the building for restoration it was decided that a replica building would have to be built in its place, circa 1960. DM

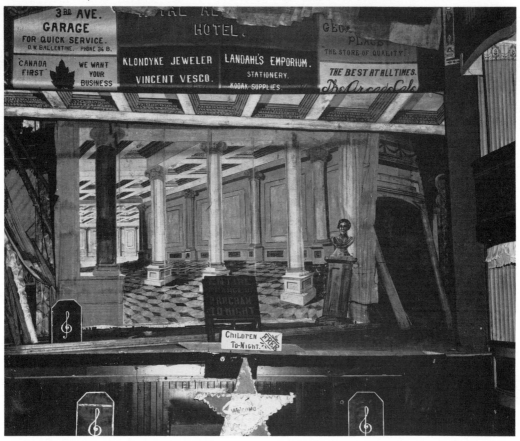

Principals of the opera
"Patience," April 24-26, 1905.
UAA, RALPH McKAY COLLECTION

The play "Captain Swift," per-
formed April 1, 1907. DM

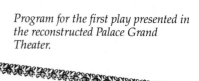

Program for the first play presented in the reconstructed Palace Grand Theater.

The Palace Grand Theater was called The Savoy from Aug. 1900 to Sept. 1901. UW

The Palace Grand as it appears after the 1962 reconstruction. Today the Gaslight Follies sponsored by the K.V.A. is one of the highlights for visitors to Dawson. YG

KVA
KLONDIKE VISITORS ASSOCIATION

Klondike Visitors Association

▼

Today a visitor to Dawson is touched in many ways by the Klondike Visitors Association (K.V.A.). It has grown from humble beginnings in 1952, in an attempt to revitalize the sagging economy of Dawson, to its world reknowned status of today.

When Canadian Pacific (CP) Air in 1954 began running the steamer *S.S. Klondike* to take tourists from Whitehorse to Dawson on the Yukon River, the K.V.A. decided to meet each landing with local volunteers in Gay '90s costumes and put on their variety show, "Klondike Nights." The boat ran only for a couple of seasons but "Klondike Nights" continued. Until 1962, the entertainment and organization was conducted by volunteer members. Then professionals were hired to produce the show at the newly reconstructed Palace Grand Theater.

In 1971 the Yukon Territorial Government gave the K.V.A. permission to conduct a limited gambling operation in Canada's only legalized gambling hall, the present Diamond Tooth Gertie's. During the first years the dancers in the nightly stage show worked all day and donned can-can costumes at night. As the business continued to grow, the first paid employees were hired in 1975.

In today's highly concentrated visitors' facilities in Dawson, the K.V.A. operates Diamond Tooth Gertie's Gambling Hall, the Gaslight Follies at the Palace Grand Theater, the Gold Room above the Canadian Imperial Bank of Commerce, Jack London's Cabin and Interpretation Centre and Claim #6 on Bonanza Creek. It sponsors or co-sponsors the Spring Carnival, Dawson City Gold Show, the Commissioner's Ball, Yukon Goldpanning Championship, the International Dome Race, Yukon Talent Night, Mixed Slowpitch Baseball Tournament, the Great International Outhouse Race and the Klondike Open Dart Tournament. The K.V.A. also owns the Oddfellows Hall and the historic Gun and Ammo Shop.

Two full-time staff members, with C. Holloway as general manager run the K.V.A., hiring 80 to 90 people during the tourist season.

CHAPTER FOURTEEN
PEOPLE OF DAWSON

Portrait of Dawson members of Yukon Order of Pioneers in front of the Pioneer Hall, early 1950s. PABC

YUKON PIONEERS

Robert Henderson. UW

These four men were responsible for the discovery of the fabulous Klondike gold strike in August 1896. George Carmack, Skookum Jim and Tagish Charley actually discovered the gold after being directed to Rabbit Creek (now called Bonanza Creek) by long-time northern prospector, Robert Henderson.

George Carmack. UW

Skookum Jim. YA

Tagish Charley. YA

William Ogilvie was the official surveyor for the Canadian government and surveyed the boundary between Alaska and the Yukon. He had the reputation of being the most honest man in the North, never wanting any personal gain for himself, and was named the Commissioner of the Yukon in 1898. UW

YUKON PIONEERS

Yukon Order of Pioneers (YOOP) on Discovery Day, Aug. 17, 1912. DM

Lodge members of Dawson Lodge, No. 1, I.O.O. F. stand in front of their new permanent home on April 24, 1910. DM

Group photo of the Grand Lodge of the Yukon Order of Pioneers in Whitehorse. Back row, left to right: John Gould, Father Bobillier, Brud Cyr, Bill Drury. Front row: Mike Comadina, Frank Lidstone, Elmer Gaudrone and G.I. Cameron, 1971. DM

The fourth contingent of Canadian volunteers leaving Dawson for overseas service in front of the Dawson Administration Building, Oct. 9, 1916. DM, C. TIDD

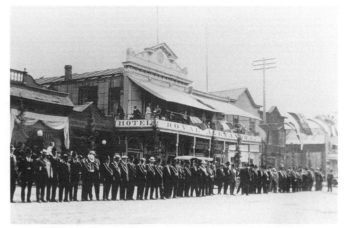

Exterior of the hotel on the east side of Front Street with some people on its second story balcony. A receiving line of about 59 YOOP's on Front Street is in the foreground. Taken on Discovery Day, 1922. DM

A group photograph of about 20 men and women on the Dome to watch the midnight sun. One man has a camera, June 21, 1899. DM, HEGG

Group of 10 well-dressed men posing in front of a log building, 1909. DM, ELLINGSEN

Midnight photograph of a social gathering at the Commissioner's residence honoring the Seattle Chamber of Commerce. DM, DOODY

Dawson City Chapter I.O.D.E. reception for Mrs. George Black (wife of commissioner of the Yukon), July 29, 1922. DM, ELLINGSEN

PERSONALITIES

Percy DeWolfe, "Iron Man of the North," hauled mail along the Yukon River between Dawson City and Eagle, Alaska from 1915 to 1950. Most of his summers were spent at his fish camp about 25 miles downstream from Dawson. DM

A Moosehide native and her son. AUTHOR'S COLLECTION

"Big Alex" McDonald, one of the gold rush's most well-known personalities. He first came to the Yukon in 1895 to Fortymile. He had enormous success in the gold fields and amassed a fortuhe, which earned him the title "King of the Klondike." He was a very generous man, who helped his fellow miners, and contributed to many civic causes. However he died a pauper in 1909 after making $20 million during the gold rush period. AMHA

WOMEN OF DAWSON

Kate "Klondike Kate" Rockwell lived in Oregon for many years. This early 1950s photo shows her still expounding her legend although she lived as a recluse. YA

Klondike Kate was one of the most famous of the dance hall girls of Dawson. She often wore expensive gowns and a headdress of lighted candles. After the rush was over she went on the lecture circuit, telling of her life during the gold rush days. She died a recluse in Oregon in 1957. YA

Lady of the Gold Rush in the Klondike. PAC

Four women of the 'White Chapel' or prostitution district posed on a ladder with a man drinking on the roof. Photographer's caption: Climbing the ladder of virtue.
PABC, LARSS & DUCLOS

WOMEN OF DAWSON

Ladies of the night enjoying themselves in front of their cribs at White Chapel or Klondike City. There have been camp followers in every gold rush and mining town, and the Klondike was no exception. UW, LARSS & DUCLOS

WOMEN OF DAWSON

"One of the Girls." YA.

Lucille Elliot, also known as "Swedish Queen." AMHA

A woman referred to as one of "Dawson's Favourites" seated next to the bed in her cabin. Wallpaper, prints, dresser and mirror table, dishes and assorted Victorian bric-a-brac are visible, 1898. DM, HEGG

Diamond Tooth Lil, born Honora Ornstein, may well have been the last of the Dawson dance hall girls. Her pose may seem a bit gross but to the lonely miners of early Dawson, she was one of their "sweethearts." She made and lost several fortunes and died in 1975 after spending the last 40 years of her life in mental institutions. UW

This was what Dawson was all about—a stop-over for the gold-crazed prospectors heading for the Klondike gold fields.
UW

CHAPTER FIFTEEN
BIRD'S EYE VIEWS

Early 1900s view showing the NWMP barracks, Administration Building, Court House, Commissioner's residence and St. Paul's Church. UW

AUTHOR'S COLLECTION

Downtown Dawson during World War II. Taken from a military overflight.
RANDY ACCORD, FAIRBANKS, ALASKA

A panorama of Dawson taken from directly across the Yukon River, 1943.
DM, W.S. HARE

CHAPTER SIXTEEN
MISCELLANEOUS VIEWS

Sign board on Ridge Trail above Dawson, 1899. GA, GORDON CHANDLER COLLECTION

Klondike City, across the Klondike River from Dawson, was the site of an old Indian salmon camp and was known as "Lousetown." In the early 1900s it was the site of a large sawmill. UW, CURTIS

The "ladies of the night" caused problems and they were moved to their own district, called "Oshiwora," "White Chapel" or "Lousetown," at Klondike City, across the Klondike River from Dawson. There was only a narrow footbridge to carry customers across the river. UW, LARSS & DUCLOS

Carlin's team hauling wood on skis during the winter. The ferry tower on First Avenue is visible in the background to the left with the Dawson City Hotel to the right. GA, ELLINGSEN

A flower garden in West Dawson. The long summer days produced good growing conditions. DM

West Dawson was settled, circa 1899, by people wanting to avoid overcrowding and typhoid outbreaks in Dawson. Farms also became established and later, as mining in the Sixtymile area increased, a link with Dawson became necessary. In 1902 a ferry guided by a cable began operating. This cable was supported on the opposite bank by a 37 meter tower which provided clearance for the riverboats.

Paddock's Garden in West Dawson. AUTHOR'S COLLECTION

Yukon men from Dawson who joined the Canadian army, July 1918, for service in World War I.
AUTHOR'S COLLECTION

Cemetery on the hill above Dawson, 1901.
UW, GOETZMAN

The old Indian village of Moosehide just west of Dawson in 1900. The Han Indians had a summer fish camp at the site of Klondike City prior to the gold rush. With the influx of prospectors the Han moved to the site of Moosehide by the summer of 1897 and were granted 160 acres as a reserve. The population of Moosehide decreased slowly through the years and all remaining natives had moved to Dawson by the late 1950s. YA

CHAPTER SEVENTEEN

DAWSON TODAY

DISCOVERY CLAIM
CONCESSION DE LA DÉCOUVERTE

The names Robert Henderson, Skookum Jim, Tagish Charlie
and George Carmack are inextricably linked to the discovery
of gold on Bonanza Creek. Henderson was the first to systematically explore the gold bearing potential of the region, only
to have the major find elude him. Then on 17 August 1896
Jim struck gold, and with his companions Charlie and
Carmack staked the first claims. A few days later at Forty
Mile, Carmack in his own name registered the Discovery
Claim where this monument stands. Within days Bonanza and
Eldorado Creeks had been staked and when the news reached
the outside the Klondike Gold Rush was on.

Robert Henderson, Skookum Jim, Tagish Charlie et George
Carmack sont intimement liés à la découverte de l'or dans le
ruisseau Bonanza. Henderson fut le premier à explorer systém-
atiquement le potentiel de la région, mais la découverte prin-
cipale lui échappa. Le 17 août 1896, Jim découvrit de l'or et
jalonna avec ses compagnons Charlie et Carmack les quatre
premières concessions; à Forty Mile, Carmack enregistra à
son nom la concession de la découverte où s'élève ce monument. En quelques jours, les concessions des ruisseaux
Bonanza et Eldorado furent jalonnées. Ce fut le départ de la
ruée vers l'or du Klondike.

Historic Sites and Monuments Board of Canada.
Commission des lieux et monuments historiques du Canada.

Government of Canada · 1982 · Gouvernement du Canada

The site of the first gold discovery on Aug. 17, 1896, on
Bonanza Creek, about 12 miles from Dawson City.

The ferry dock on Dawson's west end.

Looking west across the Yukon River and the road leading to the Alaska border.

Third Avenue looking south.

Dawson today.
GOVERNMENT OF
THE YUKON

Some of the new buildings along Front Street.

Third Avenue looking west with the giant earth slide (Moosehide Slide) on the hillside above town.

One of North America's most famous authors, Jack London, took part in the Klondike gold rush. He went north in 1897 to seek his fortune along with thousands of others. After taking the dangerous trip through Miles Canyon and the White Horse Rapids, he floated down the Yukon River but wintered at Stewart River, just a day's run from Dawson City, as ice closed the Yukon. Here he soaked up the tales of the Yukon that later built his literary reputation. He spent some time in Dawson the next summer but decided that mining was not for him. This cabin, which was discovered in 1965 by Dick North and others on the Left Fork of Henderson Creek, had London's name written on a log inside. London had lived in the cabin for a time in early 1898. It was decided the cabin should be taken apart, hauled to the Yukon River and divided up, with two identical cabins being built from the logs. One would be reconstructed in Dawson City and the other at Jack London Square in Oakland, California, London's hometown. Both cabins were rebuilt in 1969. Today the Dawson City cabin is a major tourist attraction. An adjoining visitor's center has an exhibit of photographs and readings of London's stories are presented in the summer months by Dick North, well-known Northern author and Jack London researcher. The K.V.A. built and operates the attraction.

Dawson Daily News *building.*

Buildings on Third Avenue between King and Queen streets. Caley's Store, on the right, was built in 1899 or 1900. It contained several stores and a boarding house until 1907 when it became a lodging house known as "The White House." It was a hotel in the early 1920s and a general store operated by Frederick Caley in 1948.

The post office at the corner of King Street and Third Avenue.

The back of the post office held the Dominion Telegraph office at one time.

The Commissioner's residence on Front Street between Church and Turner streets. The exterior has been restored but much work remains to be done on the inside. Tours are conducted through the residence.

The Canadian Bank of Commerce building before the outside covering was added. AMHA

The impressive Canadian Imperial Bank of Commerce building on the waterfront opened in 1901. It is a frame building, asbestos-lined against fire, with ornamental iron work painted to resemble stone. It had Dawson's first flush toilet system. The bank's 90-year lease was up in 1988 and the building was sold. The bank moved to a new location.

Diamond Tooth Gertie's Gambling Hall is housed in the old Arctic Brotherhood Hall.

Can can dancing and a floor show are a nightly feature in Gertie's—bringing back the flavor of the gold rush days.

An old garage that apparently sold Chevrolet cars at one time.

The Yukon Saw Mill at Front and Duke streets. One of the largest mills built at the height of the building boom, it was closed in the late teens. The building was used as a cold storage warehouse in 1931 and was later owned by the Northern Commercial Company.

The old Carnegie Library building was built in 1904 with a
$25,000 grant from the Carnegie Foundation. It housed the
Dawson Free Library until 1934 when it was purchased by
the local Masonic Lodge. The frame building is covered
with metal to simulate stone work.

West Machine Shop—from 1900, a restaurant until 1903,
then a freight business until 1907, also a saddle shop and
after 1929 a machine shop. Now demolished.

Strachans Grocery on Second Avenue was not quite
straight with the rest of the world from many years, but is
now being restored.

Close-up view of the front door of the old Carnegie Library.

Strait's Auction House at the
corner of Third Avenue and
Harper Street is one of the
most photographed buildings
in Dawson. Ebenezer Strait
opened his auction business
here prior to 1900. He dealt
in a number of commodities
including secondhand items.
In 1972 the building was
given to the Klondike Visitors
Association. Although the
building is in a deplorable
state, it did survive the
disastrous 1979 flood.

Harrington's Store was built in 1900 and housed W.A. Harrington & Son grocery store. The business closed around 1915 and in 1950 the building housed a bicycle repair shop. Parks Canada restored the building and it now houses a historical photograph exhibit.

The Yukon Hotel at Front and Church streets was a log building completed in 1898. The Federal Government leased the building for offices and it became a hotel in 1909. It was first known as the Freeman Hotel and then as the Miner's Rest until 1934 when it was renamed The Yukon Hotel. It is now restored and contains apartments for senior citizens.

Red Feather Saloon at the corner of Third Avenue and Princess Street. It was built around 1902 and operated as "The McDonald Saloon" until 1909, when its name was changed to "The Hub." It became "The Red Feather Saloon" in 1914 but closed in 1917 due to prohibition. It is now demolished.

The Dawson Hardware Company on Second Avenue. The sign and facade date from 1901, however the rest of the building is of more modern vintage.

This house, on Fifth Avenue across from the museum, was built in 1901-02 for Superintendent Cuthbert, commanding officer of the NWMP.

Winault's store was built in 1902. Stores in the building in 1903 included a shoemaker, barber, the Standard Circulating Library, a restaurant and the Monarch Shoe Company. Upstairs were furnished rooms. It was the Oak Hall Clothing Store in 1905-06, then a men's clothing and shoe store in 1909. Herbert Winault bought the building in 1932 and operated a general store until the late 1940s, when it was purchased by J. Butterworth. Butterworth operated a store here until 1957.

St. Andrew's Church on Fifth Avenue and Church Street has been ravaged by time. The interior floor has buckled from the underlying frozen soil.

St. Mary's Catholic Church on Fifth Avenue and King Street was constructed in 1904. The Catholic school occupied the first floor with the church above it. The school closed in 1966 but the church is still in use. The belltower was added in 1924 to house an 1,150-pound bell brought from the first Catholic church which closed in 1923.

Klondike Kate's Restaurant is located in a building across from the old post office. It dates from 1901.

St. Paul's Church was built on Church Street in 1902 to replace the first Anglican Church on the site, built in 1897. St. Paul's was built for $15,000, $12,000 of which was provided by area miners.

Madame Tremblay's Store at Third Avenue and King Street was built in 1899 at the corner of Fourth Avenue and King Street and moved to its present site in 1905. In 1913 it was purchased by Jack Tremblay, a prominent local miner. Madame Emilie Tremblay operated a dry goods store until 1936. It is still a dry goods store.

The Dawson Visitor Reception Center on Front Street should be a visitor's first stop in historic Dawson City. It is a replica of the Northern Commercial Company's building which stood here from 1897 until 1951.

The old curling club was formerly a cold storage warehouse for the Northern Commercial Company. It was one of four built in 1898. The curling club moved to its new site in 1981.

One of the few buildings left from the old NWMP headquarters is this stable, built in 1903.

Time and soil conditions have not been kind to some of Dawson's buildings.

The Bank of British North America at Second Avenue and Queen Street is being restored by Parks Canada. The bank came to Dawson in 1898 and a permanent building was erected here but was destroyed by fire in 1899. Alex McDonald owned the building and had his real estate and mining office here until 1905. The Bank of British North America bought the building in 1910 and the Bank of Montreal, which took over the Bank of British North America's assets in 1919, operated from here until 1968.

The Court House along Front Street is now Canadian Parks Service Administration office.

Due to the constant threat of floods (the 1979 flood wreaked havoc in town), the government built this dike along the Yukon River in the late 1980s.

Waterfront view showing the S.S. Keno and the Canadian Imperial Bank of Commerce. This photo was taken before the dike was built.

This sign is just to the west of Whitehorse.

Several old locomotives, used on the Klondike Mines Railway, are on display next to the Dawson City Museum. They are now under a wooden shed.

Views of the S.S. Keno, one of three steamers on display in the Yukon, sits on the shore of the Yukon River. It was built in 1922 and plied the river until brought to her final resting place in 1960.

The "Queen City of the North" can be seen in all her summer glory from the Dome above town. Its population today is about 800 residents compared to over 30,000 at the height of the gold rush.

THE PHOTOGRAPHERS

Photographers whose photos appear in this book:
Adams & Larkin
Barley, H.C.
Cantwell, George
Chisholm, _____
Curtis, Asahel
Doody, J.
Ellingsen, E.O.
Finnie, Richard
Gillis, Dr. A.J.
Goetzman, H.J.
Haines, C.
Hegg, E.A.
Keir, _____
Larss & Duclos
Norvell, _____
Nowell, F.H.
Tidd, C.
Vogee, Arthur
Wolfe, _____
Woodside, _____

Other photographs are credited when known.

Clarke and Clarence Kinsey were prolific photographers of Dawson and the nearby mining town of Grand Forks. DM

Larss & Duclos studio in Dawson. PAC

Main Street, 1898, showing the studio of prolific gold rush photographer, E.A. Hegg. UW

George Mercer Dawson
1849-1901

George Mercer Dawson was born in Pictou, Nova Scotia on Aug. 1, 1849. He was the eldest son of Sir William Dawson, who later became principal of McGill University, and Margaret Mercer. In 1855, when George was six years of age, his family moved to Montreal where his father began his tenure at McGill. Four years later, at the age of 10, George contracted what is now believed to have been polio. As a result of this illness, his growth was stunted and his spine became permanently deformed.

Despite his physical weakness George went on to become one of the most eminent geologists of his day. He undertook numerous expeditions under conditions of great physical hardship. His endurance and courage were admired by all who worked with him. In 1873 and 1874 Dawson explored the 49th parallel from Lake of the Woods to the Pacific coast, as geologist and botanist to Her Majesty's North American Boundary Commission. Among his many other expeditions were those to Northern British Columbia and the Peace River region (1875, 1879); the Queen Charlotte Islands (1877, 1878); and the Yukon (1887, 1888). Thus Dawson was in the area of what is now Dawson Creek in 1875 and again in 1879. Dawson Creek along with Dawson City in the Yukon, were named in his honor. George Dawson was a man of many and varied accomplishments. Not only was he a geologist, but also a naturalist and archaeologist. His contributions to our knowledge of the languages and customs of many Canadian Indian tribes have justly earned him the title of "Father of Canadian Anthropology." Nor were his achievements limited exclusively to the domain of science. He was a photographer, an artist and somewhat of a minor poet.

Dawson made a companion of the Order of St. Michael and St. George by Her Majesty Queen Victoria. He also received honorary degrees from McGill, Queen's and Princeton Universities, and was the holder of numerous scientific honors and awards. At the time of his death, March 2, 1901, George Dawson was director of the Geological Survey of Canada and president of the Geological Society of America.

Selected Bibliography

Archibald, Margaret, *A Substantial Expression of Confidence: The Northern Commercial Company Store, Dawson, 1897-1951*, History and Archaeology 63, National Historic Parks and Sites Branch, Parks Canada, Environment Canada, Ottawa, 1982.

_____, *Grubstake to Grocery Store: Supplying the Klondike, 1897-1907*, Canadian Historic Sites, Occasional Papers in Archaeology and History 26, Ottawa, 1981.

Becker, Ethel Anderson, *Klondike 98, Hegg's Album of the 1898 Alaska Gold Rush*, Binfords & Mort, Portland, Oregon, 1949.

Berton, Pierre, *Klondike, The Last Great Gold Rush, 1896-1899*, McClelland and Stewart Ltd., Toronto, Ontario, 1972.

_____, *The Klondike Quest, A Photographic Essay, 1897-1899*, Little Brown and Co., Boston, 1983.

Bolotin, Norman, *A Klondike Scrapbook, Ordinary People, Extraordinary Times*, Chronicle Books, San Francisco, 1987.

Bronson, William, *The Last Grand Adventure, The Story of the Klondike Gold Rush & the Opening of Alaska*, McGraw-Hill Book Co., New York, 1977.

Cohen, Stan, *The Streets Were Paved With Gold, A Pictorial History of the Klondike Gold Rush, 1896-1899*, Pictorial Histories Publ. Co., Missoula, Montana, 1976.

Doogan, Mike, *Dawson City*, Alaska Geographic, Volume 15, Number 2, Anchorage, 1988.

Lung, Edward Burchall, *Black Sand and Gold*, 1956.

Morgan, Murray, *One Man's Gold Rush, A Klondike Album*, University of Washington Press, Seattle, 1967.

North, Dick, *Jack London's Cabin*, Volume I, Willow Printers, Whitehorse, 1986.

Sack, Doug, *A Brief History of Dawson City and the Klondike*, Privately Printed.

Summer, Harold Merritt, *This Was Klondike Fever*, Superior Publishing Co., Seattle, 1978.

Winslow, Kathryn, *Big Pan-Out: The Story of the Klondike Gold Rush*, W.W. Norton & Co., New York, 1951.

Wright, Allen A., *Prelude to Bonanza, The Discovery and Exploration of the Yukon*, Gray's Publishing Ltd., Sidney, British Columbia, 1976.

THE KLONDIKE NUGGET.

VOL. 1 No. 47   DAWSON, Y. T., WEDNESDAY, JUNE 14, 1899   PRICE 25 CENTS

FIGHT LOST ON A FOUL.

KLONDIKERS LEAVE FOR CAPE NOME.

Off on a Two-Thousand-Mile Stampede to the Coast.

The end of the gold rush and a new beginning for Dawson City began with the discovery of gold on the beaches off Nome, Alaska in the summer of 1899. COURTESY STEPHEN GOLDMAN, PARKTON, MARYLAND